PARENTS, PREDATORS, AND PREVENTION

The complete guide to keeping your kids safe and confident

SECOND EDITION

By
Sergeant James Giammarinaro

First published by Pelican Press in 2006

Second Edition published in 2008
by Child Safety Team, Inc.

ISBN 13: 978-1-888562-18-7
ISBN 10: 1-888562-18-8

Printed in the United States of America

Child Safety Team, Inc.
St. Augustine, Florida
www.childsafetyteam.com

DEDICATION

This book is dedicated to the victims and their families. Losing a child is tragic. Losing a child to abduction and murder is an unspeakable horror. In my home state of Florida, there were three recent cases of innocent, young girls being raped and murdered. You cannot imagine the suffering and raw emotion until it hits close to home.

I further dedicate this book to the Law Enforcement Agencies and volunteers, all working together with the highest degree of compassion and cooperation, in a concerted effort to find these abducted children before it is too late.

Finally, this book is dedicated to all those parents committed to protecting and educating their children, to prevent them from becoming future victims.

ACKNOWLEDGEMENTS

Special thanks to…

My TaeKwonDo Instructor and good friend, Master Mark Holanchock, of North Florida Martial Arts, for all he has taught me, and for all he does for the young people of St. Augustine, Florida. Master Holanchock has been a mentor to me for the past eight years, and he continues to inspire me and all those around him.

To the Keshner Family for their effort and their unwavering friendship. Without them this book would not be possible.

To Matthew Altonbach of Vision Quest Photography, who provided the professional and creative photographs for the front cover and for the self-defense techniques…a job very well done.

To the children and adults who modeled for the photographs in this book, providing true-to-life visual images.

Most of all, to my wonderful wife, Tonya, and to our children, for their tireless patience, loyalty and support.

TABLE OF CONTENTS

PARENTS, PREDATORS, AND PREVENTION

The complete guide to keeping your kids safe and confident

From the Author

Dear Reader,

It seems that every time we turn the TV on, and watch CNN or the local news, or open a newspaper, we are assaulted by the gut-wrenching scene of parents pleading for the safe return of their missing child.

We immediately understand what these anguished parents don't want to believe - that they will never see their child alive again. Adding painful insult to horrible injury, these same parents will be forced to learn the sickening details of exactly how their child suffered during his or her final hours alive, before being cruelly murdered.

This is a sick and scary world we live in today: a little girl repeatedly raped, then buried alive clutching a stuffed animal; a son abducted by an estranged parent, and never heard from again...

Tragically, many of these incidents need never have happened if only we could know how to create a safer environment for our children...if only we could teach these little people who we love most how to reduce the chances of their becoming victims, how to recognize danger, and how to react if they are ever confronted by one of these sick predators.

This book was written with the hope that you, the parents and teachers, will take the time to learn how best to protect your children. I hope that you will come away from having read this book able to make a major difference in the future safety of your child. And that you will discuss what you have learned with other parents and teachers, and most importantly, with your children.

Sincerely from a concerned parent,

Sgt. James Giammarinaro

St. Augustine, Florida.

INTRODUCTION

> *You're in the house making your child and his friends a snack as they play in the cul-de-sac of your safe and quiet neighborhood. Smiling as you watch them play, you turn away from the kitchen window, secure in the knowledge that the kids are having harmless fun. Suddenly you hear the sound of squealing tires and kids screaming. You get a sick feeling in the pit of your stomach as you run out the door...the kids are screaming and pointing, a car is speeding down the street...just like that, your worst nightmare comes to pass, your 8-year-old boy has just been abducted.*

Could this happen to you and your child? Most of us would confidently say, "No, my child is safe from harm...those kind of things don't happen where I live."

Think again. Yes, it could happen to you and your child. Every year, thousands of children are taken by a stranger, and many are never returned. Of those abductions, many occur in middle to upper class neighborhoods that experience little to no crime. Tragically, many of these abductions could have been prevented through the teaching of Situational Awareness Programs.

I am a veteran Police Officer with over seventeen years experience in Law Enforcement. I am currently a Sergeant with the St. Augustine Police Department in St. Augustine, Florida, and I teach such safety awareness programs.

I became interested in children's safety eight years ago, when I started taking TaeKwonDo with my son. I moved up the ranks to black belt, and then started teaching this martial art to both adults and youth. I especially enjoyed working with children, and watching how TaeKwonDo helped youth to be strong and self-confident, and to become aware of potential dangers.

This combination of my law enforcement background and martial arts training emphasized the need for safety awareness. It provided a new perspective on self-defense - particularly regarding children. I began to feel a special obligation to keep children safe...to give them the skills and knowledge they would need to protect themselves in the event of an attempted abduction.

For the past five years, I have taught safety awareness programs to kids in schools, summer camps, church groups, Boy Scouts, 4-H clubs, martial arts students and other groups, gaining valuable experience along the way from these kids - especially regarding the safety information they receive, or don't receive, from their parents. I realized that, as good as our youth programs are, they fail to target the audience who matters most: you, the parents.

During EVERY safety awareness program I've taught, I've been amazed to learn that only 50% of the youth present have ever been warned about 'Stranger Danger', or taught any kind of safety awareness. As a police officer who has seen first hand the dangers children face, I am appalled at this number. I cannot believe that most parents have not taken the time to sit down with their children and talk about the most important topic in the world.

I am not saying this as an insult to parents. I understand that we all have busy schedules, and we may take for granted that our children know some basic safety rules. But, the truth of the matter is, the majority of children either doesn't know, or chooses not to follow them. Either way, the worst thing parents can do is *assume* their children know how to stay safe. We need to *be sure* they know – it's our job to teach them.

So…this guide is intended to help you do just that. My goal is to empower every parent I can reach to keep his or her children safe from predators. With my knowledge, our mutual passion, and a little bit of time and commitment, we can prevent your child from becoming a statistic. I can't think of a better way to spend our time.

While doing research for this book, I heard something that rang so true that I must share it with you: "Younger children listen, but do not understand; and older children understand, but do not listen." It is our job as parents to make them both listen and understand.

AREN'T YOU GLAD THAT PARENTS TAKE THE TIME TO WATCH THEIR KIDS THESE DAYS?
PEDOPHILES PERVERTS& CHILD ABDUCTORS

Unless commitment is made,
there are only promises and hopes; but no plans.
~ Peter F. Drucker ~

CHAPTER 1
PARENTING AND COMMITMENT

Parenting – choosing to have a child and agreeing to take care of that child for at least eighteen years – is a commitment. This course of action starts the day you bring your child home from the hospital and will continue well into the future.

What is the definition of commitment? Commitment is the act of binding yourself (intellectually or emotionally) to a course of action. Commitment is the agreement or pledge to do something in the future. Commitment means never giving up! No matter what or how hard the challenge, if it's worth having, it's worth the effort.

Every child has his or her own personality and demeanor, and some are more stubborn and defiant than others. I know this for a fact - I have three children of my own. As you well know, at some point, your children will begin to test your commitment level to see if you just give up and let them have free reign. This is when you have to be strong and stick to your plan for raising your child in a safe and confident manner, no matter how much he or she pushes back. You will probably feel like nothing is sinking in, but a day will come when your child tells you, "Thanks for never giving up on me."

Let's be honest though, it is not a perfect world, and there are many different types of household dynamics, with more kids being left at home alone than ever before while their mother or father works; and many children are raised in a single parent environment. This, however, should increase the level of a parent's commitment to a child. In today's world, parents need to teach their children more than just the difference between right and wrong. When kids are left alone with little or no supervision, the difference between right and wrong can become blurred and confusing. Left to their own judgement, it is fairly easy for kids to make a mistake that could be life-threatening. These circumstances make it crucial to talk to and instruct our kids about how to keep safe from predators...on the streets, in our neighborhoods, on the Internet, and even knocking on our doors.

Parents must be committed to teaching safety, by: maintaining a constant dialogue concerning the dangers they face; actively listening to their kids' conversations; being aware of what is going on in their kids' lives; and proactively circumventing danger by role-playing possible abduction situations. Role-playing is one of the best prevention tools a parent can use, and it will be discussed in detail in Chapter Five.

Just remember one thing: if you do not talk to your children, keeping an open line of communication - someone else will; and, believe me, there are plenty of predators out there looking for the child who is lacking a solid parental relationship at home.

One is not exposed to danger who,
even when in safety, is always on their guard.
~ Publilius Syrus ~

CHAPTER 2
EDUCATE YOURSELF AND YOUR CHILDREN

What would you do if you or your child had a serious disease? Actually, the question should be, "What wouldn't you do?" You would go to the ends of the earth to find a cure, anything to save your child. Preventing the horror of an abduction from happening is proactively no different.

We all know doctors or lawyers, and how many years of schooling they have to complete before they are given the legal right to make life and death decisions in their important professions.

To me, however, the most important job in the world is being a parent. We receive no formal training, nor do we need a license to practice this huge responsibility of having and raising a child. Policemen see the negative effects of poor parenting on a daily basis. I believe that Parenting Classes should be a mandatory prerequisite before giving birth. Instead, new parents have only their own parents to learn from – and, in many cases, they are far less than adequate teachers.

Many times parents have the best intentions, and think they have educated themselves and taught their children how to stay safe. A statewide poll of 625 parents, conducted in Florida by **Mason-Dixon Polling and Research** between June 19-22, 2006, found that:

> "Florida parents perceive their children to be at greater risk than ever before as they go out in the community, rove the World Wide Web, or participate in after school programs and summer camps."

One of the poll questions was, "Have you or have you not instructed your child/all your children in what to do when approached by someone they don't know?" 97% of the parents polled said they "Have."

However, while conducting Situational Awareness Seminars, I like to ask children to raise their hands if they ever talk to their parents about 'Stranger Danger' or other safety issues, or if they know what a "Secret Password" or "Code Word" is, or what it can be used for. In response, I see a lot of blank, confused and embarrassed stares, and – in every seminar I've conducted – **approximately 50%** of the children raise their hands. Think about that number: out of every group of 100 children, about 50 of them have never spoken to their parents about safety issues. That number is unacceptable, and it completely contradicts the Mason-Dixon poll.

Clearly, the message is not getting through. Almost 100% of parents *say* they instruct their children about safety and situational awareness, yet less than 50% of children in our seminars agree. This is a perfect example of how crucial it is to be **sure** your kids listen, hear and understand how to be safe. Just saying, "Stay away from strangers" doesn't cut it in this day and age.

This is the reason why I decided to write this book – to give parents an effective, common sense approach to safety awareness that their children will listen to and learn. Hopefully, after reading the book, parents will share the information with a friend. We must learn to work together to defeat this evil. As you learn how to keep your children safe and confident, please pass the information along. This topic is not a secret recipe which we lock in a safety deposit box. We want everyone to learn so that the perverts, pedophiles and offenders have nowhere to go, no one to hurt.

How can parents educate themselves?

That's an easy one. Read this book! All kidding aside, there are many ways to educate yourself about safety awareness:

1. Know the Facts:

According to the *National Incidence Studies of Missing, Abducted, Runaway, and Thrownaway Children* (NISMART-2, released in October 2002), which studied the year 1999, an estimated 797,500 children were reported missing; 58,200 children were abducted by non-family members; 115 children were the victims of the most serious, long-term non-family abductions called "stereotypical kidnappings"; and 203,900 children were the victims of family abductions.

An abduction involves the taking of a child, either by force or pretence, for some specific purpose such as sexual abuse, ransom, etc. An abduction does not necessarily mean that your child is gone forever. In many cases, the child is only taken for a few hours, abused and dropped off somewhere or returned home.

"Stereotypical kidnappings" are the tragedies you hear about. 115 is a relatively small number compared to the total number of children reported missing every year, thankfully because most of the 'incomplete' abductions don't make the news. However, *ONE* stereotypical kidnapping or abduction is one too many. Who can ever forget the horror of hearing of any of the following child abduction cases:

- Samantha Runnion (5 years old), Stanton, California, 2002, abducted in her front yard, raped and murdered.

- Elizabeth Smart (15 years old), Salt Lake City, Utah, 2002, kidnapped from her home in the middle of the night and taken to be raised as a second wife – thankfully returned home safely nine months later.

- Carlie Brucia (11 years old), Sarasota, Florida, 2004, abducted at a carwash, raped and murdered.

- Jessica Lunsford (9 years old), Homosassa, Florida, 2005, abducted from her home, raped and murdered.

• Sarah Lunde (13 years old), Ruskin, Florida, 2005, abducted from her home, raped and murdered.

• Jamie Bolin (10 years old), Purcell, Oklahoma, April 2006, lured into a neighbor's apartment, raped, murdered and mutilated.

• Clay Moore (13 years old), Bradenton, Florida, February 2007, was abducted from a bus stop and left tied up in the woods. Clay Moore was one of the lucky ones - he was able to escape to safety.

• Christopher Barrios, Jr. (6 years old), Glynn County, GA, March 2007, was abducted walking home from a neighbor's house, by a registered sex offender. Christopher Barrios was raped and murdered.

2. Do the Research:

In Law Enforcement, certain situations place unlimited resources at our disposal. A missing child case is one of those situations. I have never seen people come together so quickly and professionally, and work together as a team as well as they do when it involves crimes against children. Because of this community effort over the past few years, many organizations have formed to combat child abduction, and their websites provide invaluable information:

-The National Center for Missing and Exploited Children, www.missingkids.com. They can be contacted at 1-800-THELOST, or 1-800-843-5678. This agency does wonderful work. They have information, books, and brochures about all kinds of topics relating to child safety awareness, and it is all free.

-www.beyondmissing.com, where Law Enforcement and parents can create and distribute missing child flyers; founded by Marc Klaas after the abduction and murder of his 12-year-old daughter, Polly.

-Sex Offender Registry - if you live in the state of Florida, and are concerned about sex offenders in your area, go to www.fdle.state.fl.us, and click on sex offender database. If you live outside the state of Florida you can go to the National Sex Offender Registry Website: www.nsopr.gov; or www.familywatchdog.us and click on 'Find Offenders.'

-www.amberalert.gov - the home of "Amber Alerts," early warnings of missing children, founded as a legacy to 9-year-old Amber Hagerman who was kidnapped and murdered in Arlington, Texas.

-In Florida, on July 19, 2006, The **SAFE STEPS** initiative was launched by the Office of the Attorney General of Florida, the National Center for Missing & Exploited Children (NCMEC), the Florida School Boards Association, Macy's, and Royal Caribbean Cruises Ltd., to help parents and guardians keep children safer from predators — in neighborhoods and on the Internet. The web site is www.safestepsfla.net.

"The critical factor is equipping parents with solid information and tips based on facts and not simply the perception of risks," said Florida Attorney General Charlie Crist.

All of these websites and organizations are excellent resources, and I encourage you to go to them and educate yourself. Read up on everything you can get your hands on, add them to your 'Favorite Sites' on your computer – and refer back to them often; then share the knowledge with your children.

If you still have questions you can always contact your local Police Department or Sheriff's Office to find out who the offenders and predators are in your area, and to see whether the police have any safety awareness programs for parents and/or children to attend.

How do you educate your children?

It's all about communication – the two way street of sharing information, and actively listening to our children to be sure they understand the message. Be aware of what is going on in their lives. When you do this, you are then able to communicate with them in a way that will not embarrass or demean them. Once you have educated yourself on how to keep your child safe, then you can educate your child. There are several ways that you can do this:

1. You can contact your local Law Enforcement Agency to see if there is a safety awareness program that you can both attend.

2. You can sit down and discuss topics with your child using aids such as books or videos.

3. You can develop a secret password together and discuss when and how to use it. (Discussed in detail in Chapter 4).

4. Of major importance is role-playing, that is, coming up with different scenarios which fit your child's environment. Role-playing is where you play one person and your child plays the other, and you act out various scenarios, and discuss how your child should respond in the most correct, safest way. You should be creative and realistic. This "game" will give your child examples to go by, allowing him to build self–confidence and good decision making skills.

Whenever I see an article in the newspapers, or an Internet reference to an attempted or actual child abduction, I save it and use it as an example. You could sit down with your child and critique the good or bad things the child did, and what your child should or should not have done in the same situation. This, to me, is the best way to get your child to understand the seriousness of the topic.

5. You can enroll them in a Martial Arts program that emphasizes awareness and self-confidence.

When educating your child, another important thing to remember is the need to set limits and to have rules and expectations. Believe it or not, most children appreciate structure and like to know their boundaries, so don't be afraid to set them. Once you have established ground rules, and have a plan in effect, it will be a lot easier to talk to your child. They will realize that you are up to date on the times and lingo. You will earn instant credibility and your children will be less likely to want to defy you.

One question I am asked a lot is, "How old should my child be before I can start talking to them about 'Stranger Danger'?" My answer to that is, as soon as they are able to talk and to communicate. You can just start out by praising them when they make a smart safety decision, and by talking frankly about the dangers they face.

The rest of the chapters in this book will address specific hazards and dangers, and explain how to prepare your child to avoid, and, if necessary, to deal with them.

"DO WE PUT HER IN A VAULT?"

Out of this nettle, danger, we pluck this flower, safety.
~ William Shakespeare ~

CHAPTER 3
SITUATIONAL AWARENESS
(formerly known as 'Stranger Danger')

In April 2006, in Purcell, Oklahoma, a ten-year-old girl was murdered and mutilated by a neighbor who lived downstairs from her. Upon contacting one of the investigators in the agency where this took place, I learned that the girl knew her killer. This story is a little more complicated than most abductions and murders, in that the girl was forced to stay home alone much of the time because her dad was a single parent and had to work to support them both. While her dad was working, the girl became friendly with her neighbor. This neighbor-turned-killer would leave the door to his apartment open and lure the local kids into the apartment by showing them his pet rat. The 10-year-old girl would also, on occasion, use the killer's phone to call for pizza.

On the tragic day in April 2006, the killer put into motion an almost year-long fantasy of abducting, killing and cannibalizing a person. He did this by once again luring the 10-year-old girl into his apartment and carrying out his fantasy as he struck her in the head with a wooden cutting board, then raped and murdered her.

Law Enforcement Officers noticed his overly nervous behavior at a traffic checkpoint, and brought him in for questioning. He eventually confessed, telling Law Enforcement that he had stuffed her body in a plastic tub, then put her inside the closet of his apartment. He actually had an online diary of his thoughts explaining how he had fantasies of killing and eating a human being. According to Law Enforcement, the killer had no prior history, but displayed signs of depression, being unable to deal with society, and he could not hold down a steady job. These are all some indicators of a potential molester/abductor.

This case is sad for several reasons, for there were a lot of things that were not done which might have prevented it. I am sure the father of the child feels crushed, because he blames himself for not being home to protect his child. However, there are many families worldwide who have similar situations, and it is the parent's job to educate their children on such dangers. Unfortunately, if this father had instructed his daughter to stay home and lock the door until he came home from work, the tragedy might have been prevented. The father also should have instructed his daughter to never go inside someone else's home unless he gave her permission and had previously met the person.

It is easy to second guess this incident, but it is just another example of how easy it is to lose our precious children if we do not take the time to educate and communicate with them. Reviewing these cases is how we learn.

We are powerless to change the heart and mind of a pedophile or to rid the world of these dangerous humans; but we can talk to our children and prepare them for the possibility of being approached by a bad guy.

Contrary to popular belief, there is no practical profile of an abductor, and if you were to ask your child what a dangerous stranger looks like, you might get an answer describing a monster with three eyes and green slime oozing from its mouth, or the spooky dirty old man in a black trench coat.

This method of teaching our children about 'Stranger Danger' is no longer acceptable or practiced. Instead, it is much more important to teach our children to respond to situations, rather than to focus on the type of person who might hurt them; so our message is now known as 'Situational Awareness'.

Recent history of abductions and murders show that the abductors are not total strangers that look scary, or the dirty old man staring from a park bench; they are defined as normal/average looking everyday people who appear harmless. They usually know their victim in some capacity, live and work in the area, have built up some type of rapport with him or her, and know the victim's patterns and schedule. In fact, in 80% of all abductions, children are taken by immediate or extended family.

Unfortunately, in this day and age, the bad guy can be anyone. ANYONE. I realize this is a broad and frightening generalization, and that's my point. Every person your child meets for the first time is considered a stranger, such as the mailman, the ice cream truck driver, the pizza man, the cable guy, the lawn service guy, etc…and, every adult your child comes into contact with has the potential to be a predator – simply because the bad guys are drawn to professions that put them in close contact with kids.

This is scary, I know, but the likelihood that your child's scout leader, teacher, or youth counselor is a bad guy is extremely low; however, as a parent, you must be on guard, so that if any situation arises that makes your child feel uncomfortable about a person, you can act accordingly.

There are basically two kinds of strangers: the good/harmless kind and the bad/dangerous types.

1) **Good Strangers**: these are normal, everyday, hardworking people with genuinely good intentions, such as: police officers, store security guards, firefighters, moms and dads with their kids, people in uniforms, or someone simply working. If a person is working, he usually does not have time to abduct your child.

2) **Bad Strangers:** these are the bad strangers/pedophiles/offenders/abductors. They are defined more by their actions than by their looks.

- Bad strangers are the people who are always thinking of new and creative ways to lure our children into a situation that is to their advantage.

- Bad strangers/abductors are defined characteristically as having low social competence, are less likely to be married, and have poor interpersonal and social skills.

- Bad strangers will go out of their way to make inappropriate contact with children when there is no legitimate purpose, such as parking in front of schools, bus stops, parks, or neighborhoods.

- Bad strangers are the people who will offer candy, toys or money to younger kids to lure them away or to keep a bad secret.

One of the best resources I have found concerning child safety is the National Center for Missing and Exploited Children, www.missingkids.com. This site shows photos of missing children and offers a place where you can report sightings of them.

Also, the site provides references for parents and Law Enforcement alike. One of the books that they offer is called, *Child Molesters: A Behavioral Analysis*. This book provides references to certain behaviors consistent with molesters/offenders.

I've listed some of these characteristics of a possible bad stranger/molester/offender on the following page, plus added more from additional references.

It is important to understand that just one of these indicators alone does not mean that a person should be labeled an offender.

Characteristics/Behaviors Common to Most Predators

1. Frequent and unexpected moves - when the person is finally identified, he is usually asked to move on, which alleviates the problem for one neighborhood, but creates it for another.

2. If the person is older than 25, single and never been married - again this indicator alone should not be a red flag.

3. If the person lives with his parents.

4. If you notice the person showing excessive interest in your child – if you notice a person wanting to spend more time with your child than with you, it's probably a good time to start worrying and paying very close attention.

5. Limited peer relationships – this goes hand and hand with poor interpersonal and social skills.

6. If the person identifies with children better than adults - a trait that is very scary because this type of person knows how to listen to and seduce children; and is more likely to seek out professions where he'll have direct contact with children, such as: a coach, a teacher, or a school bus driver.

7. If the person has access to children – this is one of the most important indicators. The person that simply hangs around areas and places where children frequent.

8. If the person volunteers or plans activities with children that include being alone with the child, such as camping trips, or hiking; or simply suggests that parents take some

time for themselves, while the pedophile will volunteer/ sacrifice to watch their child.

9. If the person seduces your child with attention, affection, and gifts – this is a very common seduction trick/technique that abductors use. They befriend, pay attention to, and buy gifts for the child which creates a bond, and develops good feelings toward the offender. For younger children, the bad guy may use candy, toys, or money as a lure; in older children, he may even use beer or drugs.

10. If the person acts like a child when around them, or allows the child to do questionable or inappropriate things.

11. If the adult does not have any children of his own, and is up to date on the most recent fads and popular music.

12. If the person asks for assistance - this is just another lure to get the child away from her friends or a public place. Instruct her to never separate from her friends, and put herself in a situation where she is away from other people.

13. If the person uses fear tactics – the person may use a weapon or threaten the child. Instruct your child not to leave a safe area even with the threat of a weapon. Tell her to yell as loud as she can in order to draw as much attention as possible. The bad guy is not going to stick around to wait for someone to identify him. He will find the quickest escape route and take it.

I am by no means saying that if you know a person or have observed a person that has some of these traits, that he - or she - is automatically a pervert and a pedophile. All I am suggesting is that you pay much closer attention to that person as well as your children, and if you recognize these indicators, the red flag should go up.

You could go on the websites provided and check to see if a suspicious person is a registered sex offender. If he is not listed, this could mean one of two things. One - you are wrong and have overreacted; or two - he just has not been caught yet. Either way, if someone makes you feel uncomfortable, you could always contact your local Law Enforcement Agency, and just make them aware of the person.

Always trust your gut instinct, if you check the person out discreetly and you are wrong, then you have not lost anything. If you don't check the person out and something happens, you will never forgive yourself.

Being able to tell the difference between good and bad strangers is next to impossible at first glance. Strangers who are predators are experts at disguising themselves.

- Predators are like chameleons. They appear in many shapes, sizes, and disguises.

- Predators can appear attractive, interesting, charming or awkward.

- Predators can be your nextdoor neighbor, your lawn man, a relative, or a co-worker.

- Predators are usually intelligent and creative.

- Predators are devious and unethical, and they have no conscience. They will stop at nothing to lure a child.

- **Predators step in where parents are absent.**

This last fact is the most frightening of all, mainly because it is so pervasive. Millions of kids out there spend too much time alone, and are starved for attention, kindness and guidance. Predators are far from stupid, and they know exactly what to say to a lonely child. Kindness and attention are what seduces children, and initially, pedophiles tend to treat children better than most adults would. They listen to their problems and concerns, and fulfill their physical and emotional needs. If a child isn't getting this kind of attention at home, it's understandable how he or she would be attracted to someone showing such attention.

Obviously, the concept of 'Stranger Danger' is confusing and full of pitfalls. When I was a child, I remember my parents and relatives teaching me to respect and pay attention to any and all grown ups, to mind my manners, and to do what I was told. Wow, have times changed! Could you imagine what would happen in today's environment if these same rules applied? Any grown up could drive up to your child and say, "Hey kid, jump in my car and I'll take you home." Taught to obey elders, the child would go. Obviously, in today's world, we cannot allow our children to be that unsuspecting and obedient anymore.

The greatest problem is trying to teach our children to be respectful and to trust people, yet on the other hand, explain to them that if someone makes them feel uncomfortable, or gets too close, that it is okay to become defensive and say, "Stop, don't come any closer!" This may be difficult to explain to some children, but it is a must. Find a way to teach your children to be respectful, yet, at the same time, teach them to be safe.

My parents also told me that if we became separated, to just stay put. This is another outdated instruction. Bad guys were taught the same thing, so when the child stays put, they send a signal saying, "I am lost, scared and vulnerable." So the bad guy will walk up, act concerned, and ask your child if he can help find his or her parents.

Instead, it would be better to instruct your children that if they become separated or lost, to go find a <u>good stranger</u>

who can then help them find their parents. Also explain to your children that if a stranger approaches and asks them to go somewhere, it is okay to say "NO." Even if they are scared about being alone, they should be more scared to go anywhere with a stranger.

Most abductor/molesters are male, so teach your child to first look for the good stranger who is also a woman - the female grocery clerk working behind the cash register, the mom in the park watching her kids play, the mom at the bus stop watching her kids get on the bus, etc.

If we give our children the tools to be safe, which have been provided in this book, I feel that they will be able to make good decisions on what is appropriate behavior for adults and what isn't; and once they decide that, then they will know what course of action to take; either stay, or run, yell and tell.

One pet peeve of mine is when I am in uniform and I hear a mom or dad say to their child, "If you don't listen to me, that officer is going to arrest you;" or "If you don't stay close to me, the boogey man is going to get you and you will never see your mom and dad again." I hear these types of statements far too often, and they concern me greatly because they send mixed signals to children.

First, this type of threat does not teach kids the difference between good and bad strangers. How do you describe what the boogey man looks like? Secondly, I just finished explaining that police officers are the good guys. If we teach our kids that the police are going to arrest them, or give mom or dad a ticket if the kids don't sit in their car seats, do you really think they would willingly approach a policeman if they needed help? Most likely not, since they have already been taught that cops are bad, and that they are going to arrest them.

Threatening children with arrest or the boogey man is obviously NOT a good approach. Children should be taught that a policeman is a good stranger, someone to reach out to in times of trouble.

At the end of this chapter, speak to your children about what a stranger looks or acts like - you may be surprised at the answer.

Also, this would be a great opportunity to open the lines of communication to see if any adults in your childrens' lives make them feel uncomfortable.

PRACTICE WAYS YOUR CHILD CAN PROTECT HIMSELF
Pretend I'm someone you don't know: "Hi! Your mom asked me to pick you up from school today."
What's the password?
"Password?"
You don't know the password. I'm NOT going with you!
DONNELLY

For safety is not a gadget, but a state of mind.
~ Eleanor Everet ~

CHAPTER 4
PASSWORD-PROTECT YOUR CHILD

We've all heard of password protecting computers, accounts, websites, etc., but **the most crucial password you as a parent can ever create is the one to protect your child**. As I discussed in the last chapter, dangerous strangers are hard to define. So how can you protect your child from a possible predator?

One very good and extremely effective safety device is the secret password. A secret password is nothing more than a word that only you and your child know, that is used in emergency situations.

For example: let's say that you and your son go to Wal-Mart and he wants to go to the toy department, and you have to go to the grocery department. You separate. Although we all know it's not the safest thing in the world to do, most of us do it anyway because it sure makes shopping easier on us parents.

Let's say that while in the milk section, you slip on some water by the coolers and fall and break your leg. Now you are incapacitated, screaming in pain, and your child has no idea what has happened to you. You are not in any position to go get him, so you send a store employee with a nice blue vest to go get your son.

The employee finds your child and tells him what happened, and your son blindly goes with the clerk, and you and your boy are reunited. Pure good luck.

Let's turn that around for a second and say that you didn't really fall and break your leg; yet a 'store employee' with a nice blue vest - someone working who is supposed to be a GOOD stranger - approaches your son, and says that his mom fell, and that she told him to come get you. Your child dutifully goes with him, and the abductor pretending to be a store employee leads your child out of the store and takes him to his car.

If this were to happen, do you think you would ever see your child again? Statistics say no. According to a 1997 study by the National Center for Missing and Exploited Children, 74% of the children that are victims of stereotypical abductions are murdered within three hours of the abduction.

So, what's the answer? How could your son have known the difference between the real and the pretend store employee?

THE SECRET PASSWORD
When the store employee asked the boy to go with him to see his mom, the first question the child should have asked was, "WHAT IS THE SECRET PASSWORD?"

It is our job to make sure that we tell our children that if a person approaches them, no matter what situation they are in, they should ask for the secret password.

Then, if the person does not know the secret password, regardless of what excuse they make, your child should yell as loud as he can, "HELP! STRANGER! FIRE! POLICE! DON'T COME ANY CLOSER!" etc., and then run as fast as he can and find a good stranger.

There is an old saying, "It is easier to ask for forgiveness than to ask for permission." In other words, your child can always apologize later if the person was legitimate; but, if he goes with the stranger with no questions asked, he may never speak again. This sounds pretty harsh, but it is reality.

The Secret Password can be used for any situation where you need to let your child know that an unusual circumstance is happening **with your consent**. For instance, you are unable to pick up your daughter from dance class because your car breaks down, and you ask a friend to pick her up instead. Even in this seemingly safe scenario, a password should be requested by your child, and known by the friend.

In another scenario, your car breaks down, and you can't reach anyone to pick up your daughter. She's standing outside the studio waiting for you, and a predator stops in front of your child, tells her that he is a coworker of yours...that your car broke down...that you sent him...etc. The only way your daughter would know if the man is legitimate is to ask him for the Secret Password.

The importance of this simple safety device cannot be overstated. Make it a game that your child loves to play. Set up realistic situations where your child can practice using the Secret Password. Remember a child's short attention span and memory, and that repetition is essential.

Let us not look back in anger or forward in fear,
but around in awareness.
~ James Thurber ~

CHAPTER 5
ROLE-PLAY FOR SAFETY

While doing Situational Awareness Seminars, what I hear many times from parents is that they don't want to frighten their children. I don't believe that exposing kids to reality is scaring them; I believe that this empowers them. Knowledge is power - the more our children know and are aware of the dangers out there, the more confident they will become, and the better they will be able to deal with situations as they arise.

Studies show that most middle-upper class kids are naïve, and are more at risk to being abducted than lower-class children. This is true, not because of class, but because children raised with more street experience are more aware of their surroundings. They have not been sheltered from reality.

Parents try to shelter children from all that is bad and ugly in this world, but truth be told, doing so only hampers their ability to grow as people, and it dulls the awareness of their environment. **Because children face so many dangers today; AND because these dangers are so difficult to recognize, responsible parents cannot afford to shelter their children. The stakes are too high.**

Instead of hiding from dangers, face them head on by role-playing dangerous situations with your child. Create scenarios based on your specific environment, and his or her unique personality. Enlist the help of friends and family to play the roles of the bad guy, the good person to go to for help, etc. Practice these scenarios constantly so that they become etched in your child's mind. Then, when a similar situation occurs, your child will have the knowledge needed to make an intelligent, informed decision. Also, the more you practice, the more the proper reaction becomes instinctual, meaning the child acts in a smart way without having to even think about it. It's just like everything else we do in life. The more you do it the better you become at it.

The following scenarios are good ones to begin role-playing with. They are a few of the more common ploys used by predators.

Scenario # 1 – The Puppy Ploy

Your daughter is playing alone in the front of your house, and a stranger approaches her and asks for help finding his puppy. Appealing to a child's love for animals is a common ruse used by abductors and predators.

In this scenario, you should teach your daughter to run inside and "yell and tell" an adult about the stranger. Make sure she knows that, in this situation, it is okay to be mean to that person if she is scared.

"What about if my neighbor asks my daughter for help finding an animal, and she knows the neighbor and the animal?" you may ask. Again, your child should run inside and tell you what is going on. Also, why would your neighbor, if well-intentioned, ask a child to search for a lost animal without the parent's permission?

Scenario # 2 – An Adult in an Auto

a) Your son is walking down the street, or is in front of your house and a car pulls up and asks for directions.

The first question he should ask (in his mind) is, "Why is a grown person asking me for directions?"

It does not make any sense for an adult to ask a child for directions, it is just a ploy to get him close enough to the vehicle to grab him. Instruct your son to stay far away from the car, and tell the stranger that he will go inside to get his mom.

b) An adult pulls up and calls your daughter by name, and says, "Your mom or dad asked me to pick you up." How do you think the bad guy knew your child's name? Check her backpack or clothing. Does it have her name on it? If so, remove it. Knowing a child's name gives the bad guy instant credibility. If you want to mark your child's items, use a patch, sticker, or mark that only you and your child will recognize.

In this situation, the secret password is huge. All your daughter has to do is ask for it. If the person does not know the password, then instruct her not to go with the adult to the car, and immediately turn around - turning as far away from the car as possible - and run the opposite direction the car is facing, and find a 'good' adult.

If the person tries to get out of the vehicle and come toward your daughter, instruct her to drop her book bag, and again, run in the opposite direction of the vehicle. Remember, **run, yell and tell**.

Tell her not to worry about the backpack, it can easily be replaced - her life cannot. By dropping the backpack, she is doing two things. First, she is becoming lighter so she can run away faster. Second, she is creating a trail to follow were something bad to happen. This will, at least, give Law Enforcement a place to start, and can be used as an article of clothing for a K-9 unit to use for tracking purposes.

Scenario # 3 – Safety in Numbers

Your son and a friend are playing together in a park, and the friend has to go home. Your child decides to continue playing. All of a sudden, a stranger walks up and asks to play with him. The stranger then offers him some type of toy, but it is in his car. This is a major no-no.

First of all, instruct your son about "Safety in Numbers" -

that he should never stay around as the last child...he should never find himself in a position where he is alone. Staying with friends can greatly reduce the chances of becoming abducted, because it deters the bad guy from targeting your child because there is a witness who could identify him and/or his vehicle.

Secondly, if your child ever does find himself alone and confronted by a stranger, that he should avoid talking to the person - no matter what the stranger says - and walk quickly or run to the nearest public place to find a 'good stranger.'

One of the most important things a person can do in these scenarios is call the police as soon as possible. In order to get these predators off the street, we have to work as a team. The sooner the police can get either a clothing description or vehicle description, the better chance they have of locating and identifying the bad guys cruising the neighborhoods.

Scenario # 4 – "You Could be a Model!"

Your daughter and her friend are walking home from school. Suddenly a man approaches with a camera. The man tells the two girls how pretty they are and that he believes that they could be model material. The stranger then advises the girls that he is new in town, and that he is starting a new modeling & fashion magazine. He is looking for a few photogenic girls, and your daughter and her friend would be perfect for his new magazine.

In this situation you should insist that your daughter and her friend turn toward the direction they just came from, and start running. They should also start yelling to draw attention to themselves...yell and tell. It is not normal for a person to just hop out of a vehicle and approach young girls in order to take their picture. If the person was a legitimate fashion photographer, he would advertise professionally, setting up times and places for the photo shoot to take place, and he would make sure that the child's parents were present and that a waiver was signed.

Remember the old saying...if it sounds too good to be true - it probably is. Once again the bad guy preys on girls, their vulnerabilities, and their dreams of becoming models. He knows just what to say to get the girls to go along with him. Although this is just one scenario, it is very important to stress safety in numbers. I know I have said this before, but besides the secret password, safety in numbers is your next best safety belt.

—

These are just a few scenarios to get you started. Use the following pages to create your own Situational Awareness scenarios to practice with your children. Remember to make them realistic according to your environment and lifestyle. Write them down so you can return to these pages and practice them over and over again.

Scenario 5: ______________________________

Scenario 6: ______________________________

____

____

____

____

____

____

____

____

____

____

____

____

____

____

____

____

Scenario 7: ______________________________

____

____

____

____

____

____

____

____

____

____

____

____

____

____

____

____

Scenario 8: ______________________________

CHAPTER 6
DO YOU KNOW WHERE YOUR KIDS ARE?

As parents, it is our job to always know our children's activities, to always know where they are and when they are due home. Know where your children are at all times; keep a list of their friends' names, addresses and phone numbers. With all our new cell phone technology, program your child's friends' phone numbers into your cell phone so you have easy and quick access to your child.

On the job, it drives me crazy when I respond to a call, and find that kids are running the streets and that their parents have no idea where their kids are. A common situation is that these kids have told their mom or dad that they were going over to Johnny's, but, in fact, they were not.

If your child says he wants to go over to a friend's house, make sure you have met the parents, and that you have their home number. You can then check up on your child, letting him know that you care enough to monitor his whereabouts.

Another contingency is where the parents do not have rules and expectations, and do not monitor where their kids go, or who they hang out with. We, in Law Enforcement, have no control over this irresponsible parenting; but we are frequently called in when these kids turn troublemakers. Neither do you, as parents, have any control over these kids. You can, however, instruct your child to stay away from them, and to never go to a friend's home if the parents are not at home.

Children left to care for themselves rarely make good choices. Try to limit unsupervised time by finding positive activities for your children to take part in, such as organized sports, clubs, youth centers, scouts, church groups, 4-H, etc. Most youth programs not only provide something to do, but they also help build confidence, social skills, maturity and responsibility.

When you are home with your child, keep an open line of communication. Let her know that she can tell you anything, that you are understanding, and are there to support her in everything she does. If you establish an atmosphere that promotes honesty, caring and open communication, your child will be more willing to come to you when a serious problem arises. If she feels like you are not going to believe or support her, or take the time to listen, then she will not approach you with anything as serious as molestation.

In 10% of all abduction cases, even if the lines of communication are open, the child does not report the crime, not wanting to get the person in trouble, because she knows the abductor, or the abductor has threatened to hurt her or a family member. This is a very tough situation, because your child loves you, and does not want to see you hurt, and she feels like she cannot say or do anything to stop the abuse.

The best that you can do is to know your child. Be aware of any sudden changes in her behavior - is she distant or irritable? Are there changes in her sleep or eating patterns? Does she have negative reactions to any adults? If so, don't overlook any of these situations, they could signal abuse happening right under your nose.

In 79% of abduction/assault cases, families do not report them to the police for fear of shame to the family, or for selfish reasons. Many abductions go unreported because of fear, blackmail, embarrassment and confusion.

I once worked a case where the stepfather sexually assaulted the stepdaughter, and the natural mother knew about it. This is a more common occurrence than you would like to think. The family pretended it was not happening. Thank God, a friend of the daughter had sense enough to tell another adult. I believe that the parents would not have done anything to change the situation otherwise, and that poor girl would have wound up thinking that it was all her fault.

Needless to say, we picked up the stepfather, and took him to jail. I believe the mom felt badly about what happened to her daughter; but was willing to sacrifice her, since Hubby was their meal ticket, and if he went to jail they would lose everything. It shocked me further when the child's mother stayed married to the pervert, and the child went to live with her real father's family.

Many parents take safety precautions with their young children, giving older children increased freedom at younger and younger ages. These parents fail to realize that older kids can easily become abduction victims as well. As a matter of fact, prior to conducting research for this book, I thought that most abductions and murders occurred to younger children; however, statistics show that the homicide rate is highest between the ages of 13 to 17, and are most likely committed by an acquaintance of the child.

Try to have your teens earn their freedom and privileges. Let them know what is expected of them. Talk to them about risky behavior, because their appearance and the way that they carry themselves makes a big difference in how the bad guys (and people in general) will perceive them.

Risky behavior can mean several different things, including drinking, drugs and sex. Yes, although we hate to talk about it or think about it, our kids will start talking about it and then ***do it!*** It is inevitable, and it is our job, to talk to our children about sex - early. Lack of communication leads to bad decisions, which may lead to abductions, rape and murder. This is a parent's worst nightmare.

Communicating with our kids, and role-playing different scenarios, will help our children learn to avoid the risky situations that drinking, doing drugs and having sex can put them into.

I can't tell you how many cases I have worked as a detective where young college girls report being raped. ALL the reports sound the same. They all start out like this:

> *My friends and I went to a bar and had a few drinks... (They had fake ID's to get into the bar, being underage to begin with) ...and I met a nice guy. We went back to his place to hang out, and the next morning I*

woke up and I felt like something happened... (I am trying to keep it clean here).

The next thing you know, they are reporting that they have been raped and we are doing a complete investigation, including a sexual assault examination.

After everything has calmed down, and everyone sits back and evaluates what happened, we usually come to the conclusion that it was probably consensual sex, but because they were so intoxicated, they just don't remember what happened. They are embarrassed and ashamed of themselves for putting themselves in that situation in the first place.

I am not saying that there are no actual cases of sexual assault taking place; but that it has been my experience that once a young girl drinks too much and follows a young man to his home...she places herself in a vulnerable position, and is more likely to become a victim. Communicating these dangers to young people **before** they happen is the key to keeping them safe and smart. Children are not born with safety skills - they must be learned. Whether aged 5 or 18, children feel their youth, their vitality...safety is the last thing on their minds.

My job is to inform parents that it is our job to communicate and role-play with our kids in order to arm them with the tools and confidence they need to make sound decisions, and to remain safe.

AND THEY CALL US MONSTERS...!
BODIES OF TWO GIRLS LOCATED
Kidnapped girl, 5, was raped, strangled
BABY SNATCHER
Teenagers abducted at gunpoint
AMBER ALERT

CHAPTER 7
THE INTERNET INTRUDER

In our modern, high-technology world, it is no longer enough to teach our children about the strangers that we meet; now we must teach them about the perverts on the Internet who connive their way into our homes. The Internet has become a high-tech mall, a place where Predators can entice and entrap our kids. It is important to monitor our children when they are on the Internet. However, before we can intelligently do that, we have to know what we are looking for.

Online Guidelines

The first step in creating a safe Internet for your child is to create a set of guidelines when it comes to using the computer/ Internet. Here are some rules to start with. Your children must:

- Always ask for permission before getting on the Internet.

- ***Never*** give out any personal information online, such as their name, address, phone number, or the school they attend. If they desire to do so, they must ask for parental permission.

- ***Never*** open or answer any e-mails or instant messages from people they don't know.

- ***Never*** tell anyone their password, which includes friends or people who appear official (except their own parents). I have seen this happen on the job, and it causes all kinds of problems, with the person receiving embarrassing and unwanted e-mails.

- ***Never*** make plans to meet people that they have met on the Internet. The person they meet on the Internet may very well be somebody totally different than who he or she has portrayed. If they meet that person alone, without telling you, they could be putting themselves in great danger. If somebody on the Internet asks to meet, instruct your children to tell you.

- ***Always*** tell you, their parents, if someone sends an inappropriate, uncomfortable or frightening email.

These are some basic guidelines that you and your children should sit down and talk about. Perhaps you could make a guideline list that is more appropriate for your family, print it out and put it by the computer so that they will see it every time they use it. This may sound corny, but kids actually like rules and guidelines, whether they admit it or not.

Online Risks

A 2003 survey of 1000 children, aged 7 to 18, who use the Internet, conducted by Symantec Corp., and reported on parenthood.com, showed that more than 80% of those surveyed received inappropriate emails on a daily basis. This junk mail includes sweepstake messages, meeting singles online, spam, and emails with links to X-rated porn sites.

When your children surf the web, enter chat rooms, or open their email, they become very vulnerable to some highly inappropriate material. The Internet is subject to the good, the bad, and the very ugly. The Internet IS the real world, and as parents, we need to caution our kids just as we would were they to be approached by someone on the street.

Three things to remember about the web is that it is: invasive, immediate and anonymous. It can be especially dangerous to our children. Some possible online threats that we should be aware of:

- Predators and pedophiles
- Pornography
- Racism and violence
- "Flaming" - rude and obnoxious people
- Gambling
- Receiving fraudulent information/scam

Profile of an Internet Predator

As I've already stated, there are many online hazards. However, the most potentially dangerous threat is contact by strangers, whether sexual or predatory in nature. Nearly every instance of Internet child luring or abduction begins with an initial relationship struck up on-line by a stranger.

We have already talked about what constitutes a stranger. You must explain to your children that anyone you meet online is a stranger, unless that person is someone they already know well in person. If you would not let your children talk to a total stranger in person, then why would you allow your children to talk to someone online who they've never met before?

The truth is that most people your children will meet on the Internet are harmless, but the evil is always out there! According to research conducted by CyberAngels.com, 22% of children from ages 10 to 13 will be approached by an online predator. That,

Moms and Dads, means one out of every five kids will be tested by evil.

Parents find it too painful to consider the possibility of their child coming face to face with a sexual predator, but it is too important an issue to ignore. As I teach in all my Situational Awareness Seminars, everyone's first line of defense is awareness; and making both parents and children aware of Internet intruders/predators is the best way to improve the odds of our children's safety.

If we as parents don't know how a pedophile builds a child's trust, there is a much greater likelihood that that child will become a victim.

Though every case is different, there are many similar approaches used by online predators trolling for children. Kids who are lonely or are new to being online are vulnerable.

I keep saying, "If you don't talk to your kids and pay attention to their lives - someone else will." Experts also caution that parents should not feel immune just because their child seems to be happy and adjusted. Preadolescents are typically at that stage of development, where, due to insecurity, their minds can be easily manipulated.

Children just reaching adolescence are becoming more mobile, able to get around more, and are becoming curious about their sexuality. They are starting to have their own mindsets and opinions. They are starting to feel that they do not like home, they don't like school, and they aren't popular enough. So begins the vulnerability stage that predators pick up on when talking to these preadolescents online. If your child is chatting online with someone who is able to manipulate him or her, your child could be in a lot of danger.

In fact, children running away from home to meet a stranger they have met online is so common these days that many Law Enforcement agencies have a dedicated unit doing nothing but trolling for predators online.

The problem is that the kids are not running away from home to meet a stranger. They are running away to meet somebody they think they can trust, someone they think they have formed some type of relationship with.

I have personally talked with several parents whose kids this has happened to, and luckily they were able to get their children back safely. However, there are too many parents out there who have never heard from their children again, whose kids were sexually assaulted and killed.

Online predators are also very patient. Once they make contact with your child, they engage in generic conversation until your child's barriers of caution are broken down. Then the predator introduces topics of a more personal and even sexual nature, such as asking about your son's sexuality or preying on his natural curiosity.

Predators will use pictures of pornography to give the impression that it is normal for children their age to be interested in or involved in sexual activities. Finally, after breaking down your son's barriers and feeding his sexual curiosity, the predator makes his move, arranging for a face-to-face meeting.

We parents must be made aware that the majority of contact with pedophiles is made online, in "real time," either in chat rooms or by instant messaging (IM). Chat sites are a great way to meet people, and they can easily be misused. You should constantly monitor your child's use of these chat rooms, as they can be manipulated by dangerous people pretending to be just another kid in the chat room.

Online predators can also gain information about your children by the screen names they choose. For example, you should make sure that when your daughter makes up a screen name, that it does not contain any identifying information or anything suggestive. For example, "Jacketscheer07" can provide a predator with a great deal of information: this girl (presumably a girl) goes to St. Augustine High. She is a cheerleader, and she probably graduates in 2007.

Some teens also have surprisingly suggestive screen names like "hotteen10," which will also attract the wrong kind of attention.

More and more parents are becoming aware of, and frightened by, the risks on the web, and feel increasingly frustrated by their inability to protect their children from the Internet intruder/predator. Even the availability of Parental Control Software doesn't help with the constant threat of more and more sophisticated hackers.

Some of these parents have decided not to allow their child on the Internet at all. Others require parental permission for computer use at all, or for visitation to specific chat rooms or websites. Another option is to place the computer in a room that is common to everyone. You should consider not allowing your children to have a computer in their rooms that have Internet capabilities.

Parent Proof

Although the Internet can be a scary thing for our children, we have more choices and tools than ever before to help keep our kids safe online. We can use a variety of methods, which include filtering, blocking, monitoring and tracking software in order to limit our children's exposure to inappropriate sites. The bottom line is if you feel like there may be a problem with your child receiving unwanted spam/ messages or inappropriate sites, just contact your Internet provider and they can guide you in further detail how to make the Internet safer.

When it comes to your child's safety, I don't think you can go too far. This includes invasion of privacy. I don't think it is such a bad idea to track chats and instant messages just to make sure that your child is safe and following the guidelines that you set out.

Technology provides us with a number of options and high-tech safety tools, but we cannot expect these to act as our babysitter. If you are paying attention to your child's habits and patterns, you will know when something is wrong.

The key to keeping your kids safe on the Internet is to recognize the possible dangers, understand the technology, and take the time to become involved in their online activities.

Chat Room Lingo

Although many parents these days are computer literate, you may still need a little help in understanding your children's Internet world and their secret language (Lingo). The following are acronyms for common phrases that are used in chat rooms. These acronyms were gathered by Symantec, an Internet security company.

- AAIK= as far as I know
- AFK = away from keyboard
- ASL = age, sex, location
- BB = bathroom break
- BBL = be back later
- BBS = be back soon
- BF = boyfriend
- BRB = be right back
- BTW = by the way

- CUL8R or CULR = see you later
- CUZ = because
- DN = don't know
- FYI = for your information
- G2G = got to go
- GF = girlfriend
- GG = gotta go
- GTFO = get the F*** out
- GYPO = get your pants off
- HW = home work
- XC = hard core
- IDC = I don't care
- IDK = I don't know
- IMO = in my opinion
- JAS = just a second
- JC = just chillin'
- JK = just kidding
- JW = just wondering
- KOTC = kiss on the cheek
- KPC = keep parents clueless
- LMAO = laughing my a** off
- LOL = Laughing out loud
- LYL = love you lots
- LYLAS or LYLAB = love you like a sister or brother
- NFC = no f*@cking clue
- NIFOC = naked in front of computer
- NM or NVM = never mind
- NP = no problem
- OMG = Oh, my God
- OTOH = on the other hand
- POS = parent over shoulder
- q-t = cutie
- ROFLOL = rolling on floor laughing out loud
- SN = screen name
- SRY = sorry

- Sup = what's up
- SW = so what
- TDTM = talk dirty to me
- TMI = too much information
- TTYL = talk to you later
- TY = thank you
- y = why
- u = you
- WTF = what the f*@k?
- w/e = whatever

I'm sure that this in not the complete list of acronyms, but it is certainly a lot more than I knew before researching this information. Hopefully you can use this list to impress your kids, and to let them know that you are not totally ignorant of their little world. This may also add credibility, and hopefully keep the lines of communications open in case they have experienced an uncomfortable situation and want to talk about it.

Warning Signs

Would you really be able to recognize signs that your child may be involved in inappropriate Internet activity? Hopefully you have been able to pick up a few good tips to help you feel more confident in your knowledge of Internet nightmares and how to recognize and prevent dangerous situations for your child.

According to Cyber Patrol's Safe Surfing Guide (www.cyberpatrol.com), the following are some warning signs that your child could be in danger.

- Hiding computer CDs and/or discs

- Changing/minimizing or turning off the computer screen when you enter the room. This is a dead giveaway, when you walk into the room and your child is just sitting there staring at the screen saver (Hello) we were not born yesterday.

- An empty Internet browser history.

- Finding pornographic files on the computer.

- Receiving letters, emails or gifts from someone you don't know

- Finding an extra Internet account on the computer so that inappropriate information does not show up on your account.

- Spending too much time on the Internet or being online late into the night. This is why I think it is important to keep the computer in a common area and have rules and guidelines.

- Changes in behavior, for example: secretiveness, sleeping problems, neglecting school work, avoiding normal social activities and/or withdrawing from the family.

These are all classic symptoms that we as parents should be aware of and deal with immediately. The longer you wait, the stronger bond your child can make with the predator, and the harder it will be to convince your child that the person on the other side of the high-tech highway is not who he says he is.

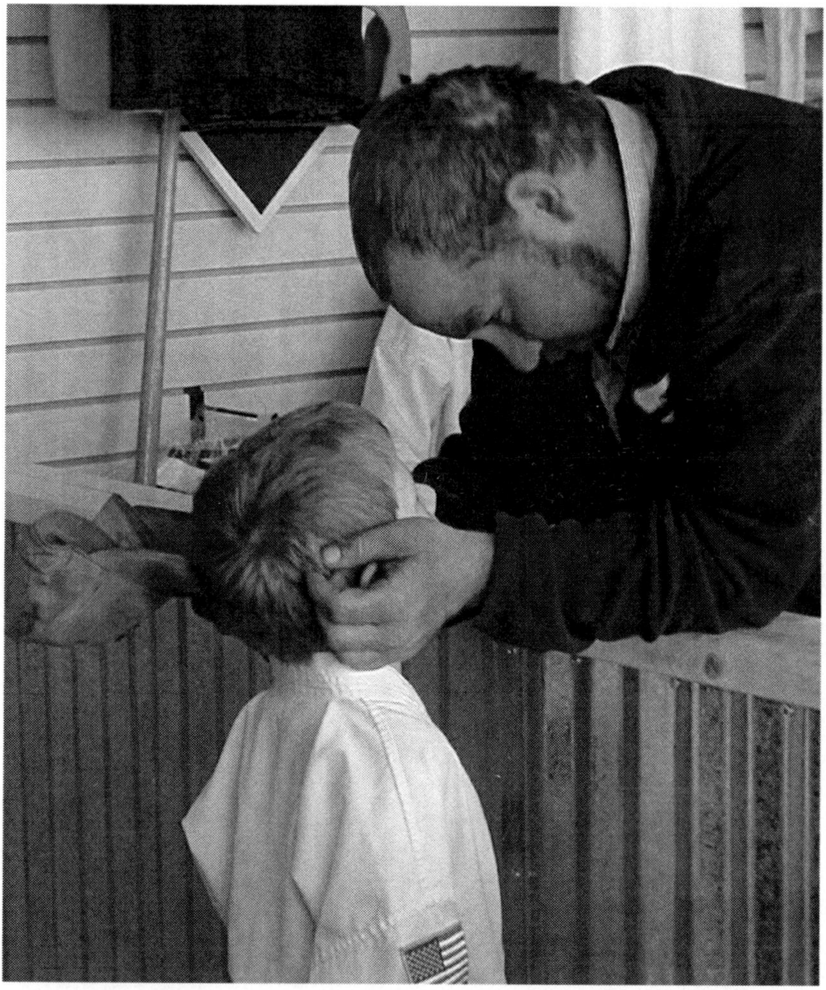

A proud, involved parent shares a special moment with his son.

It only takes a split second to destroy your life.

In every seminar I conduct, I ask children to raise their hands if they ever talk to their parents about 'Stranger Danger' - every time, <u>**approximately 50%**</u> of the children raise their hands.

Even kindergarteners get involved and ask amazing questions - it's never too early to teach safety.

Puppets help get the message across to
younger children.

This young man learns how to block an attacker
during a Situational Awareness Seminar.

"Tiny Tiger" martial arts students practice
kicking a heavy bag, which helps strengthen their kicks
if needed to defend themselves.

In martial arts sparring, young girls
gain the confidence to defend themselves.

A

B

All over the country, Law Enforcement and media team up to present mock abductions for public awareness. More often than not, the 'strangers' successfully lure the children away - shocking the parents who thought their children knew better.

In photo A, the 'stranger' manages to lure this 3-year-old girl with the promise of candy. The mother, thinking her daughter too young, had never discussed 'Stranger Danger'.

In photo B, the abduction was staged to see if the public would take action if they witnessed an attempted abduction. Several people passed by, doing nothing, before two young men finally stopped to check out the situation.

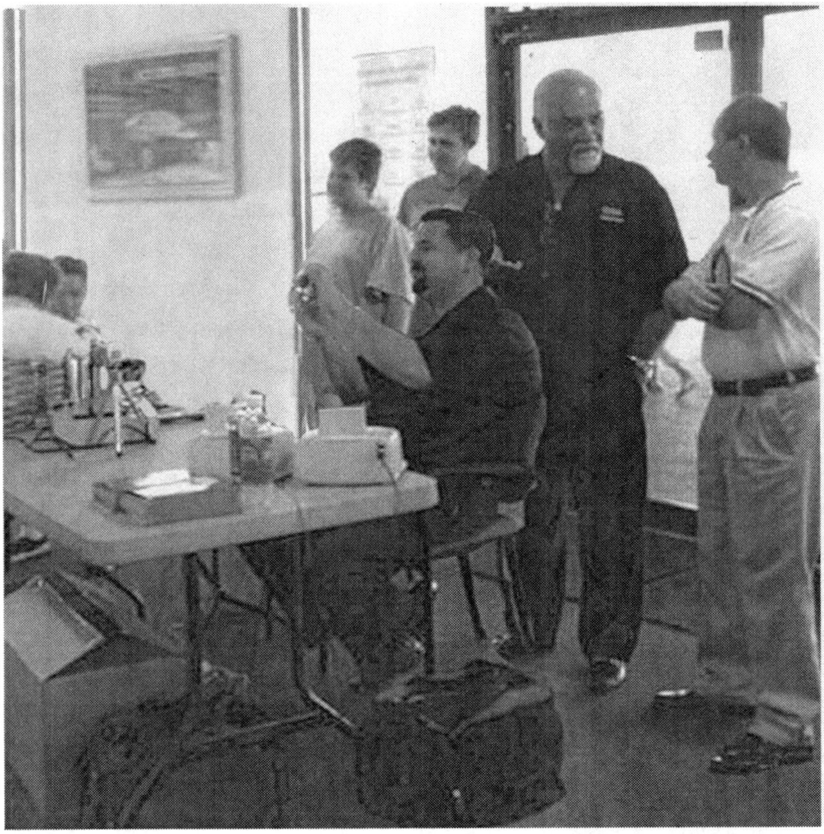

Joseph Matthews, Founder of DNA Life Print, Inc., and I team up to provide Situational Awareness and DNA Life Print Kits to the community. These DNA Life Print Kits are endorsed by John Walsh, founder of *America's Most Wanted.*

The FAMILY CIRCUS
By Bil Keane
CAN YOU ANSWER A QUESTION FOR ME, LITTLE GIRL?
NEVER TALK TO STRANGERS.
?
WHAT EVER HAPPENED TO OLD-FASHIONED FRIENDLINESS?
MOMMY! A STRANGE MAN TRIED TO TALK TO ME!
BUT I DIDN'T SAY ANYTHING...
3-14
AND I CAME RIGHT HOME.
YOU DID THE RIGHT THING, DOLLY.
I FELT SORRY FOR HIM THOUGH. HE SEEMED NICE.
WELL, HE MIGHT'VE BEEN OKAY, BUT YOU CAN NEVER BE SURE.
WE'VE NABBED HIM, SARGE! THE MOLESTER THEY'VE HAD THE APB OUT FOR!

Rather than teaching children to fear strangers, which is at best, woefully inadequate, we need to use positive messages. Children need to learn skills and confidence, not fear and avoidance.

~ Daniel Broughton ~
Former Director of the National Center for Missing and Exploited Children

CHAPTER 8
HOME ALONE

I watched a video that was produced by a local news station to test the safety procedures in place when children were home alone. Several parents took part willingly, secure in the knowledge that their children knew how to stay safe when alone. They were soon to find out differently. The children had no idea they were being 'set up,' and watched by their parents and the news cameras.

In the first scenario, the actor was a very convincing pizza delivery man. He smiled, offering the delicious pizza box, and, sure enough, the child opened the door. The parents couldn't believe their eyes. The child never stopped to ask himself the question, "Who ordered the pizza?" I guess he just assumed that mom or dad ordered it. He never thought to call mom or dad at work or on the cell phone before opening the door. Did he think the pizza fairy ordered it?

The second scenario showed an actor dressed in a telephone repair uniform. He successfully talked his way into the house to "fix the phone." The child did not check the phone to see if it was working, nor did he call his parents to see if they ordered the service.

Again, the parents were shocked. They couldn't believe that their children failed the test, nor that they hadn't listened to any of the rules they had set in place about staying home alone.

Children are, by nature, trusting and naïve, and potential abductors can be very deceiving and convincing. To a child, a pizza box and a uniform look real and unthreatening. That is why it is so important to not only teach our kids what to do when they are home alone; but to reinforce the rules over and over again until they are second nature. Kids have short attention spans, and the teachers have it right: repetition is the key to education.

Safety Rules for Children Home Alone

1. **LOCK DOORS & WINDOWS: The first and most important rule is to teach your children to keep the doors & windows locked and NOT TO ANSWER THE DOOR - FOR ANYONE!! - NEIGHBOR, RELATIVE, FRIEND'S PARENT OR SERVICE PERSON.** Also, keep the blinds or curtains closed and don't peak out. Explain to your children that they might as well invite a bad guy in for cookies and milk, because they are telling him that mom and/or dad are not home.

2. **POST EMERGENCY NUMBERS: The next most important thing to secure your children's safety is to have emergency numbers posted where everyone in the house knows where they are, preferably on the refrigerator or close to the phone**. These numbers should include Police, Fire and Rescue, and mom and dad's work and cell phone numbers.

3. **HIDE AND SEEK HELP:** If any adult comes to your house, instruct your children to **get to a phone somewhere out of view and call and tell you. If the bad guy actually breaks into the house, have them call 911 and leave the phone on and then go hide.** Role-playing can come in handy here, since you can prioritize hiding places in various parts of the house. If at all possible, tell

your children to try to escape out of a window and run to a neighbor's house, screaming for help. Make sure your children know which neighbor is likeliest to be home, and talk to your neighbor about the possibility of them seeking safe harbor with her.

4. **STRICT PHONE RULES: The phone should not be answered by a child home alone. If you need to get in touch with your child, come up with a system that is safe and easy to remember**. For instance, if you have an answering machine, call the house and instruct your child to not answer the phone until she hears your voice. If you do not have an answering machine, come up with a special code/number of rings to let your child know that it is you, and that when you call back, it will be okay to answer the phone. This system will be a little more confusing for your child, so, if at all possible, I would look into purchasing an answering machine. This is a small price to pay for your own piece of mind.

5. **ROLE-PLAY**: As I mentioned in the previous chapter on Situational Awareness – **a stranger can be anyone. Come up with scenarios you can role-play with your kids**, such as the pizza delivery person or the service person. What about the mail man? He's very likely to ring your doorbell for a package signature. Your kids may even know him – but it's still not a good idea to open the door. Tell the kids what they should do, specifically: do not let an adult in…period…then role-play the situations over and over again. Abductors are smart and creative, so it's crucial that you come up with different and realistic scenarios to see how your kids will respond.

6. **THINK AHEAD:** Do not schedule any home service while your kids are alone; nor should you have food

delivered. Plan meals ahead – why take the chance of a stranger approaching your home? You may think that the pest control guy you have had for ten years is the greatest guy in the world, but how well do you really know him? How do you know that he is not going to unlock your child's window and come back at 2:00a.m. to abduct your child? I know you are probably saying to yourself, "This guy has been a cop too long and has lost his mind;" but the truth is, these scenarios actually happen.

Such was the case of Elizabeth Smart in Utah. Her parents hired a handyman to do some work around the house. The handyman opened a window before he left; and during the night he came back and abducted her. Thank God this story had a happy ending, but it took many months to resolve itself. The abductor took Elizabeth and used her as his second wife for nine months before, finally, somebody recognized her and notified the police.

7. **STAY INSIDE:** Children home alone should stay INSIDE the house. They should not ride their bike, or skateboard, or run to the corner store.

8. **BABYSITTERS:** If your child is too young to stay home alone, be sure to thoroughly check the references of anyone you entrust to watch your child. If the babysitter is a teenager, be sure to share these same rules; and, it's not a bad idea to add a couple more rules, such as: stay off the phone or the Internet, and no visitors unless you have given prior approval.

I hope many of these instructions are already familiar to you, and that you practice them on a daily basis.

Precaution is better than the cure
~ Edward Coke ~

CHAPTER 9
BECOMING AWARE

This is one of my favorite chapters, since this is where we actually start interacting with the kids, and teaching them how to become more aware and ***empowered***. By now, hopefully, I have shared enough information with you to keep your kids safe, but I bet you are still asking yourself, "How do we *empower* our kids?" **We do so by giving our children the knowledge, strength and confidence to protect themselves – defend themselves - from bad strangers. Knowledge creates power – the power to NOT be a victim!**

A helpful way to remember the tools used in conflict avoidance and self-defense, is to break them down into **"ABCD":**

A-Awareness
B-Body Language
C-Control Boundaries
D-Defend Yourself

A – Awareness: be aware of your surroundings and look alert. You have seen other people, or perhaps even your own children walking around with their heads down, seemingly in la-la land, right? Maybe they have so much on their minds that they are just not paying attention to what is going on around them? Who do you think the abductor is going to go after? The child who appears to be daydreaming or lacking in self-confidence; or the child who is walking with her head held high, conscious of her surroundings?

Encourage awareness and self-confidence by complimenting your children when they display these traits. Your aim is to prevent them from being caught by surprise. Again, role-playing comes in handy – especially when they're daydreaming or in la-la land...catch them by surprise, show them how easy it is to sneak up on someone who is not paying attention!

An alternative method of teaching awareness is to ask them "feeling" questions such as, "Did anything or anyone make you feel scared or uncomfortable today?" Give your child a chance to feel observant. You might ask him if someone at school or in the neighborhood is being a bully? These are good questions to sharpen your child's observation skills, helping him to become more aware.

Although most of what I am saying is geared towards teaching children to be safe, parents have an obligation to hone their skills as well. Parents have a responsibility to be extremely cautious of whom they bring into their children's lives. This includes dates, co-workers, potential friends...get to know these people carefully before bringing them home. You can never be too careful.

B - Body Language: Similar to awareness, but the physical portrayal of confidence is the way a person carries himself. Teach your child to walk with his head high, shoulders back, not hunched over as if he is afraid, or lacks confidence...not to look like a victim.

Teach your child to look into a person's eyes when talking to them. My favorite Martial Arts Class to teach is the 'Tiny Tigers,' ages 4 to 6. Our first goal is to instill courtesy and confidence. I instruct the children to look someone in the eye while introducing themselves; to greet them with a firm handshake and ask for their name. I coach each child to greet a person by saying, "Hi! Nice to meet you, my name is Johnnie, what's yours?"

The child must get the other person's name and then come back to me and tell me what it is. Many new students are so afraid that they cannot do this exercise. Others attempt an introduction, but are so afraid that by the time they come back to me, they have already forgotten the person's name. It's amazing to watch these little people, after only a few classes and watching the more experienced students do it, quickly grow in confidence, able to introduce themselves to two and three people at a time and come back to me with the correct names. That is what body language and confidence can do for a person.

However, our children do not learn this on their own. They depend on us to lead by example, and to show them. Remember, constant role-playing is the key. Have them try this introduction with your friends, co-workers and other people that you come into contact with together on a daily basis. There is a difference, however, between courteous confidence, and just walking up to strangers and talking to them without your permission or knowledge. You must set rules and boundaries in order to create guidelines for safety.

B can also stand for **"Breathing to Remain Calm."** Emotion and logic do not mix. Have you noticed that you forget to breathe when you are scared or stressed out? Teach your children to take deep breaths when stressed or scared. This breathing technique will help them to calm down, and will allow them to think more clearly. I actually do a type of breathing exercise at work as I respond to an "in progress" call, if I think there is a real chance of getting into a foot or car chase or a fight. By taking long, deep breaths, and letting them out slowly, it allows your brain and your common sense to catch up to the adrenaline pumping into your bloodstream. Arriving at the scene more relaxed, hopefully I am able to think and act more clearly. This exercise really does work, but as with everything else, it must be practiced.

C – Control your boundaries: you should not allow a stranger to get close enough to be able to grab you. In police work, we call this our 'intimate' or 'personal zone,' which basically means that we do not want to let someone get so close to us that they can hit us, stab us, or grab our gun.

Are we perfect? No. Can it happen? Yes, but our goal is by putting our A, B, and C's together, we reduce our risk. Explain to your child that if he feels uncomfortable with a person getting too close, that it is okay to step back, or even to say, "Stop! Don't come any closer! Stay back!" Again, a 'good' stranger will understand, whereas a 'bad' stranger may keep coming or try to lure your child.

A recent, tragic example of this scenario, where a child allowed an adult to get close, happened in Florida in February of 2004. An 11-year-old girl was approached by an abductor behind a car wash. The abductor walked right up to the girl and led her away out of camera view and into his car. The girl was found raped and murdered two days later.

Never let your child walk alone. As stated in Chapter 5, it is so important to teach our kids that there is "safety in numbers." An abductor is drawn to a lone child like a moth to a flame.

C can also mean **"Communicating with Confidence:"** Bad guys do not have alternate plans, only alternate victims. Bad guys are going to test your child, so explain to her that tone of voice is very important. The louder, the more confident she sounds, the better. She should yell strong, clear statements, such as, "Stay Back!" or "Don't come any closer!"

D – Defend yourself: means just that. You have told your child about the dangers of strangers; you've gone over all kinds of scenarios, and taught your child to be confident and safe with the A, B, and C's of self-defense…yet still the abductor tries to come after your child. Now what? What is your child supposed to do? I tell my students that in this situation there is only one thing that you ***must never do***, and that is ***DO NOTHING!!!*** If all else fails:

HIT HARD – FAST AND FIRST THEN RUN, YELL AND TELL

Think about that for a second. You do not have to be a black belt in the Martial Arts, or be seven feet tall to defend yourself; you just have to be willing to do something…anything. Even if that means yelling, screaming, biting, kicking, etc...

Just remember this; the bad guy is looking for a weak and timid victim, one who will give up without a fight. He is not looking for the aware, confident person who is not afraid to defend herself while making a lot of noise that will attract attention.

Fear is the future of courage and the mother of safety.
~ Henry H. Tweedy ~

CHAPTER 10
TAKING ACTION

In Aurora, Colorado, a child was walking to school, when a suspect pulled up and asked her if she needed a ride and grabbed her by the arm. Another vehicle approached them, and the child pulled her arm back from his grasp and ran away, toward school. Before the suspect drove off, the child memorized his vehicle's license plate number and told school staff members about the incident when she got to school. The suspect was apprehended and taken into custody.

Attempted abductions such as this never make the national headlines. However, the National Center for Missing and Exploited Children issues a list of them every week. These *attempted* abductions aren't deemed newsworthy by the media because no one is actually abducted and murdered. To me, that is exactly what we need to be reporting - that there are children out there who are aware of their surroundings, and who are not afraid to take action in order to save themselves.

This list, which I receive weekly, shows several revealing correlations in abductions:

1. There is no age bracket within which children are safe - kids from age 5 all the way up to 17 years of age are targeted.

2. There is no preference as to the sex of the child - both boys and girls are targeted.

3. There is no single method of abduction, there are many different methods which the bad guys use in an effort to lure, or to physically grab a child. That's why it is so important to teach your child to react to many different situations rather than the way a stranger looks

4. Most of these attempted abductions occurred simply because the children were walking or playing alone and did not use the buddy system/safety in numbers rule.

5. Last, and most important, the kids who fought back - any way they could - got away.

Another thing I have noticed in many of these cases, is that persons committing crimes against children don't want to bring attention to their actions; so, as soon as a child begins struggling or making noise, they give up and leave the area in a hurry.

So, in an abduction situation, fear plays a major role - on both sides. Were you to look in the dictionary for the definition of "fear," it would read: "an emotion caused by the threat of some form of harm, promoting a decision to fight or escape, otherwise known as the 'fight or flight syndrome'."

Fear causes the release of adrenaline, which can either hurt or help us. By educating your child and giving your child a plan of action, he will be able to overcome the fear, and use the adrenaline rush to his advantage.

Fear is bolstered by ignorance, knowledge is power; so if we provide our children with tools they could easily use in the case of an emergency, we're giving them an advantage over the perpetrator who most likely hasn't given his reaction to a struggle a second thought.

By this point in the book, you, as the parent, should already have a good understanding of how to empower your children to be safe and to be able to prevent most uncomfortable or dangerous situations. However, the time may come when they might have to be more proactive than just being aware. By using true-to-life illustrations, this chapter will demonstrate just how your children could defend themselves from a would-be attacker/abductor

That said, however, **the very first thing** we should tell our kids is **to run away from a stranger/abductor as fast as they can, and to only strike somebody as a last resort.** This is not a sign of weakness, but a sign of intelligence - distance is THE best way a child can protect himself.

The next best way is through learning a few simple, yet effective, self-defense techniques. One of the overriding principals of self-defense training is to attack the softest/ weakest part of your opponent's body with the hardest/ strongest part of your own body. Men, if you have ever been hit in the groin; or women, if your child has ever accidentally poked you in the eye with her finger, then you know the truth of this statement. It's an easy enough concept that children can learn and remember.

Perhaps the hardest part is having to tell our children to think, "*Where* can I strike that will HURT the worst?" Yes, teaching such a statement goes against the basic rule of civility we're all taught from the time we're young; that's why it is crucial to discuss that self-defense is only used in emergency situations.

In TaeKwonDo training, every class begins with students reciting the Five Moral Tenets of TaeKwonDo: Courtesy, Integrity, Perseverence, Self-control and Indominable Spirit; and every class ends with students reciting the student oath, one line of which is, "...I shall never misuse

TaeKwonDo." It is very important to explain to your child that **self-defense is only to be used when he feels that his life is being threatened**, and not when Johnnie takes his seat in class, or talks to a girl he likes.

As a Police Officer and as a Martial Arts Instructor, I know the value of repeated education, role-playing and training. Hours are spent in preparation for that one life-or-death moment in life when you need to call upon all the training you have received in order to defend yourself or someone else's life. This same principal applies to teaching our children.

You pray that the day never comes, but if it does, you hope that your child will be ready. People get all worked up at the thought of actually having to defend themselves, and they think that they will not be able to do so; but the thought of the alternative - abduction, rape, murder - should clear up any doubts. Our only alternative is to fight back, and to give ourselves a fighting chance to survive. The old saying that 'anything is better than nothing' is sound advice.

The following pages illustrate nine parts of the body that your child could strike in order to incapacitate an attacker long enough to get away. The strike areas are divided into those in the upper and lower parts of the body:

Upper Parts:

-Eyes (poke person in the eyes with fingers)

-Nose (perform palm heel strike to nose)

-Neck (hammerfist, ridge hand or chop to side of neck)

-Ears (ear smash with both hands to attackers' ears)

-Throat (one or two fingers in the notch below the Adam's apple)

Lower Parts:

-Knee (strike knee with your foot - either a sidekick or a front kick)

-Groin (strike groin with knee, foot, instep or fist)

-Shin (if attacked from behind, rake the person's shin with the edge of your foot/shoe)

-Stomp (if attacked from behind, stomp on person's instep with foot/shoe)

Review these step-by-step self-defense instructions, then practice them with your child.

SELF-DEFENSE #1
EYE POKE

CHILD POKES ATTACKER IN THE EYES WITH HER FINGERS

Child shows confidence with good stance and hands up.

Attacker grabs child's arm or wrist.

Child pokes attacker in the eyes.

Child grabs own arm and pulls away (away and down).

Child turns, runs, yells and tells.

SELF-DEFENSE #2
NOSE

PALM-HEEL STRIKE: FINGERS UP, FLAT PALM - HIT ATTACKER'S NOSE WITH BASE OF PALM

Child shows confidence with good stance and hands up.

Attacker grabs child's arm or wrist.

Child strikes attacker's nose with heel of palm.

Child grabs own arm and pulls away and down.

Child turns, runs, yells and tells.

SELF-DEFENSE #3
NECK/HAMMERFIST

**CHILD STRIKES
THE SIDE OF ATTACKER'S
NECK
WITH HIS FIST**

Child shows confidence with good stance and hands up.

Attacker grabs child's arm or wrist.

Child strikes the side of the attacker's neck with a hammerfist.

Child grabs own arm and pulls away and down.

Child turns, runs, yells and tells.

SELF-DEFENSE #4
EAR SMASH

CHILD SMASHES ATTACKER'S EARS WITH BOTH HANDS

Child shows confidence with good stance and hands up.

Attacker picks up child in front bear hug.

Child smashes attacker's ears simultaneously with both hands.

Child delivers a kick to the attacker's groin.

Child turns, runs, yells and tells.

SELF-DEFENSE #5
FINGER POKE
TO THROAT

Child shows confidence with good stance and hands up.

Attacker grabs child's arm or wrist.

Child thrusts two fingers in notch below Adam's Apple.

Child grabs own arm and pulls away and down.

Child turns, runs, yells and tells.

SELF-DEFENSE #6
KNEE STRIKE

Child shows confidence with good stance and hands up.

Attacker grabs child's arm or wrist. Child strikes attacker's knee with kick.

Attacker keeps hold of child's arm or wrist.

Child grabs own arm and pulls away and down.

Child turns, runs, yells and tells.

SELF-DEFENSE #7
GROIN STRIKE

Child shows confidence with good stance and hands up.

Attacker grabs child's arm or wrist.

Child kicks attacker in the groin using knee or foot.

Child grabs own arm and pulls away and down.

Child turns, runs, yells and tells.

SELF-DEFENSE #8
FOOT STOMP

Child is not aware of attacker's presence.

Attacker grabs child from behind.

Child raises foot to...

...stomp on attacker's instep as hard as he can.

Child turns, runs, yells and tells.

These are just some basic examples of a person using the hardest parts of his body to attack the weakest parts of an adversary. Trust me, you do not have to be big, nor a Martial Artist to perform these simple actions effectively.

We demonstrate these moves to the younger children, and help them practice the moves. This is just one of the things that we do to help these kids retain information and build confidence. The bottom line is to reinforce to your child that he must do something, anything, including biting, scratching, kicking, and yelling if he is being abducted. When it comes to the safety of your child, anything goes.

Imagine a stranger walking up to your child and trying to grab him by the hand. Suddenly, your child yells, "No! Stop! Don't come any closer. Help! Police! Fire!" Then he delivers a kick to the attacker's groin, or an elbow to his nose. I believe the bad guy will let go of your child long enough for him to run away, yelling for help. That is the entire purpose behind these self-defense techniques. To teach your child to be confident and to be able to perform simple techniques that will prove effective in an effort to get away.

There are many techniques, styles and degrees of difficulties in self-defense; but, basically, the bottom line is that we must teach our kids to be confident and let them know that in certain situations it is okay to fight back. By the way, I am not promoting one martial art over any other; and there should be some kind of martial arts school nearby that can help train your child in these basics.

If your child is accosted and successfully gets away, the job is not finished. One of the most important things to remember is that the police cannot apprehend the bad guy unless they know what he looks like, or what kind of car he drives. So, although your child has been through a tough experience, it is very important that the police be given a good description of the person or the vehicle as soon as possible.

A good method for teaching your child to remember these details is to play a game in a non-stressful situation, so that were it to actually happen, your child would be able to assist Law Enforcement in catching the bad guy, and getting him off the street.

One game I play with my son, while we are driving down the

road, is the "observation game." I'll ask him if he saw the man standing on the street corner wearing the such-and-such jacket? Or, as we are going through the drive through of a fast food place, I'll ask if he observed the person's name-plate or what she was wearing? Over time, your child will become more observant, and more aware of his surroundings. These games are fun to play and they will increase awareness - for both of you.

When I was starting out as a police officer in training, I was driving in an area where the local soup kitchen served breakfast. Many homeless people were standing around outside the building.

I was new, trying to learn so much at once, and I was not very observant.

My training officer asked me, "Did you see that man holding the baseball bat?"

My reply, of course, was "no."

"Do you think he was getting ready to play baseball?" asked my field training officer.

Again, my answer was no. I felt so small, so embarrassed. I just wanted to drive to the station, park the car and quit.

Of course I didn't quit, and I quickly learned to be more observant. Hopefully, you'll play the "observation game" with your children so they can become more aware and observant too.

SHAME ON YOU!... KEEPING YOUR CHILD ON A LEASH LIKE AN ANIMAL!!
ANOTHER CHILD ABDUCTION
ACTUALLY, IT'S BECAUSE OF THE ANIMALS!

Safety is something that happens between your ears not something you hold in your hands.
~ Jeff Cooper ~

CHAPTER 11
THE GREAT ESCAPE

During an abduction attempt in Florida, a man pulled his car over and asked a boy if he wanted a ride. The boy said no, so the driver turned the car around and went after the boy. The boy ran to the nearest house, but no one was home. The boy then hid in some bushes while the man got out and looked for him. As the man got back in his car, the boy ran to another house which was occupied, and the owner was able to get the bad guy's license plate number and call the Police. The Police ran the plate, located the driver, and arrested the man.

This boy was smart. He didn't give up. He did what was necessary to be safe and to find help. Every situation is going to be different depending on the type of environment. If you live in a rural setting, it may be more difficult to run to a neighbor's house, a passing car or a local convenience store. In this situation, the knowledge of your area would be in your child's favor, so make a point of walking your area together, and make a game of finding hiding places, such as a ditch, a grove of trees, etc., where he could find a safe place to hide and wait for a stranger to give up and leave the area. Your child should then go home as quickly as possible and tell you, so you can call law enforcement to report the incident, and give a description of the bad guy and/or vehicle.

If you live in a more suburban area or big city, and your child is being chased, tell him to run back to where he just came from, or into the closest business or home. Again, make sure your child tries to get a description of the vehicle or the person, and call law enforcement as soon as possible.

Kids never cease to amaze me. Every time I do a Situational Awareness Seminar or do a self-defense class for the younger kids, the children ask both the craziest and the smartest questions I have ever heard.

One question they always ask is, "What if the bad guy gets me into his car?"

The answer is the same. "Don't give up. Do something. ANYTHING. The fight is not over until you are safe at home." This is an important reminder, because being in an abductor's car would be terrifying for a child, and there are specific things she can do to escape.

If an abductor does get your child into his car and drives away, your child should:

1. Assuming she is not blindfolded, try to pay attention to where she is going, so that if she is able to escape, she will be able to give the police directions to the place, or at least some type of landmark.

2. Jump out of the car, quickly get up and run. Yes, it may hurt, but look at the alternative.

3. Grab the steering wheel, go for the abductor's eyes, or the horn...anything to cause the car to crash. Remember, the abductor does not like attention, and trust me, if his car crashes into another car, preferably a parked car or tree, people are going to notice and come running. That is what we are looking for, anything to get someone's attention and to give your child a chance to escape.

4. Turn the car off, or grab the shifter if it is a standard.

If an abductor puts your child in the trunk of the car, your child can:

1. Depending on the model of the car, push down the back seat to gain access to the back seat from the trunk. There may also be a little pull handle from inside the trunk to open the trunk from the inside.

2. Kick out the taillights so that the people driving behind the car can see that either someone is in the trunk or that something is very suspicious and they can call for help.

Hopefully your children will live a healthy, happy life, but should something happen, wouldn't you feel better knowing that they are prepared mentally to deal with the situation? The abduction situations discussed in this book are, obviously, not everyday occurrences, and neither are some of the escape techniques; so it's up to you as the parent to set up such unnatural situations so your child will have the opportunity to practice the safe reactions.

While teaching TaeKwonDo, I can always tell which students practice at home and which do not. The student who takes it more seriously and does practice, comes to class ready to train, and appears more confident and sharp when doing the moves in class in front of classmates.

On the other hand, the student who does not take class seriously, and does not train at home, comes to class looking confused and unsure of himself. This is not because one student is born better than the other, it is simply because of practice. As with everything that we do in life, the more you do something, the better you become.

You gain strength, courage, and confidence
whenever you look fear in the face.
You must do the thing which you think you cannot do.
~ Eleanor Roosevelt ~

CHAPTER 12
REPORTING YOUR CHILD MISSING

I hope this chapter is the one that is never needed by you or anyone you care about. But if a child does come up missing, how you act and what you do next is very important.

First and foremost, **DO NOT PANIC, and be absolutely sure your child is not home:**

1. Check the house, maybe she fell asleep somewhere, or maybe she is playing a joke.

2. Check with your neighbors and your child's friends. Remember, by now, you should have your child's friend's phone number on your cell phone so that you don't have to worry about looking the number up in the phone book, wasting time.

3. Check outside the house, in the yard, in your next-door neighbor's yard...if your child is old enough, check to see if her bicycle is there.

If you still cannot locate your child, call the police immediately. There is no waiting period required for reporting a missing child, so the sooner the better.

One of the most important things you should do in the horrible event that your child goes missing is to be prepared with his vital information. The last thing you will want to do if this occurs is to answer all the necessary questions when you're in a state of panic. If you have a Child ID Kit already prepared, all you have to do is hand it over to Law Enforcement and let them take care of the rest. Have the kit readily available in an obvious spot such as your refrigerator or where you keep your important papers.

Your **Child ID Kit should include**:

1. personal and medical information

2. a description of physical characteristics, such as: birthmarks, scars, braces, glasses, etc.

3. a dental chart

4. a recent photograph

5. a fingerprint card

6. a DNA sample

The DNA sample is simple. All you have to do is get a zip lock bag and retrieve approximately 10 strands of hair from your child's brush or comb. Place the strands in the bag and store in your freezer. The second sample will be a cheek swab. All you have to do is take a Q-tip and swab the inside of the cheek for approximately 10 seconds. When you're finished, put the swab in a zip lock bag and store it in the freezer along with the hair strands. Make sure that you label the bags with your child's name and the date that you took the sample so that you don't mistake it for dinner.

You may be asking, "How am I supposed to fingerprint my child?" The answer is simple, go to your local Police Department or Sheriff's Office, and ask them to fingerprint your child, telling them what you are putting together. Depending on the department, there may be a small fee, but of course it is worth it. You should also try to remember to update your kit every 6 to 12 months, and to keep the information and photograph of your child current.

If you think that putting together a kit yourself will be too difficult, there is an easier way. You can order a complete Child ID Kit online by just typing in 'Child ID Kits'. This kit comes complete with the zip lock bags, swab, information sheet, and fingerprint ink. Again, there's a fee for this service, but, again, isn't it worth it?

Upon calling the Police, you should have the prepared ID Kit, as well as a list of all of his or her friend's names and numbers, a description of the clothing she was wearing, and recent photos of her.

Another detail you should try to remember to tell the Officer, if he fails to ask, is information about your child's patterns and favorite places. If he was frightened or upset, where would he run for safety?

When the officer takes the report, one of the first things he must do is enter your child into the National Crime Information Center personal file (NCIC). This will enable any Law Enforcement agency in the United States to identify your child.

When trying to remember the last time you saw him that day, try to be as accurate as possible. This helps determine how much time lapsed since your child was last seen. The sooner Law Enforcement can determine if your missing child meets the criteria for an **Amber Alert**, the better chance they have in locating him alive and safe.

The Amber Alert came about as the result of a 1996 kidnapping and murder of a 9-year-old girl by the name of Amber Hagerman, in Arlington, Texas. Amber was riding her bicycle when she was kidnapped and later brutally murdered. As a result, Law Enforcement joined forces with the media to broadcast early warnings, called 'Amber Alerts,' to help find abducted children.

Now a nationwide system, these messages/bulletins are broadcast by several methods, such as the print media, radio, television, message signs on highways, lottery machines and Law Enforcement BOLOs (acronym for 'Be On the Look Out'; Florida Department of Law Enforcement Certification Manual 2005, page 17). Since the program became a nationally coordinated effort in 2002, the Amber Alert has helped rescue over 200 children nationwide.

The Amber Alert is used only in specific circumstances, and has very strict requirements to prevent the system from becoming overused and ineffective.

In order for an Amber Alert to be issued, the following criteria must be met:

- Law Enforcement agency has to have a clear indication that the child has been abducted.

- The child has to be under the age of 18.

- Law Enforcement believes that the child's life is in danger.

- Law Enforcement needs specific information to distribute, such as a description of the suspect vehicle and/or suspect.

- The activation must be recommended by the Law Enforcement Agency of jurisdiction.

For further information on the Amber Alert you can go to www.amberalert.gov.

If your child was last seen at home, try to limit access for crime scene purposes. The more people that trample through your house and your child's room, the more contamination there is, and the harder it will be to look for clues or physical evidence. Check your child's room for any special or favorite items that are still there that he would never leave behind willingly, such as a favorite piece of jewelry, stuffed animal, or a special toy.

Force yourself to remain calm and try to recall any recent conversations you may have had with him in reference to anything or anyone bothering him. This includes checking the computer for any chat rooms, or emails that do not seem appropriate. By monitoring your child's communication, you can make sure that he does not get in over his head on the Internet.

As the thought of having your child become missing or abducted sinks in, you and your family must have the courage and determination to do whatever is necessary to bring him back home safely. Timing and coordination make a huge difference in the success of a search. As hard as this time may be, you should try to remember that people have walked in your footsteps before and continue to do so today, so if that traumatic day were to ever come, there will always be support for you.

There are many different groups and organizations out there that are ready, willing and able to help. Below are some web sites or points of contact:

-The National Center for Missing and Exploited Children. (NCMEC), www.missingkids.com, will enter your child into their database, and assist in making and posting signs around your neighborhood and town. The signs contain a photograph and vital statistics on your child.

-Beyondmissing.com contains links to several other websites that provide a wide variety of necessary services, such as: assisting you in coördinating search efforts; providing money for reward purposes; and putting you in touch with people who have experienced this tragedy before and can provide moral support.

-Association of Missing and Exploited Children's Organization (Ameco), www.amecoinc.org, is a national association of nonprofit organizations (both in your community and countrywide) that assist families of missing children. You can call Ameco to obtain the names of these organizations: (320) 363-0470.

Theses organizations are not the only ones out there, but they are a good starting place, and it helps in such a frightening situation to know that there are resources out there to help you, and that you will not have to go through this terrible tragedy alone.

All of these points covered in this chapter are important and necessary in the finding and or identification of a missing child. Be perseverant and persistent in the search for your child and never give up hope.

It is my fervent wish that, having read this book, your child's chances to remain safe within the loving confines of the family have been dramatically improved.

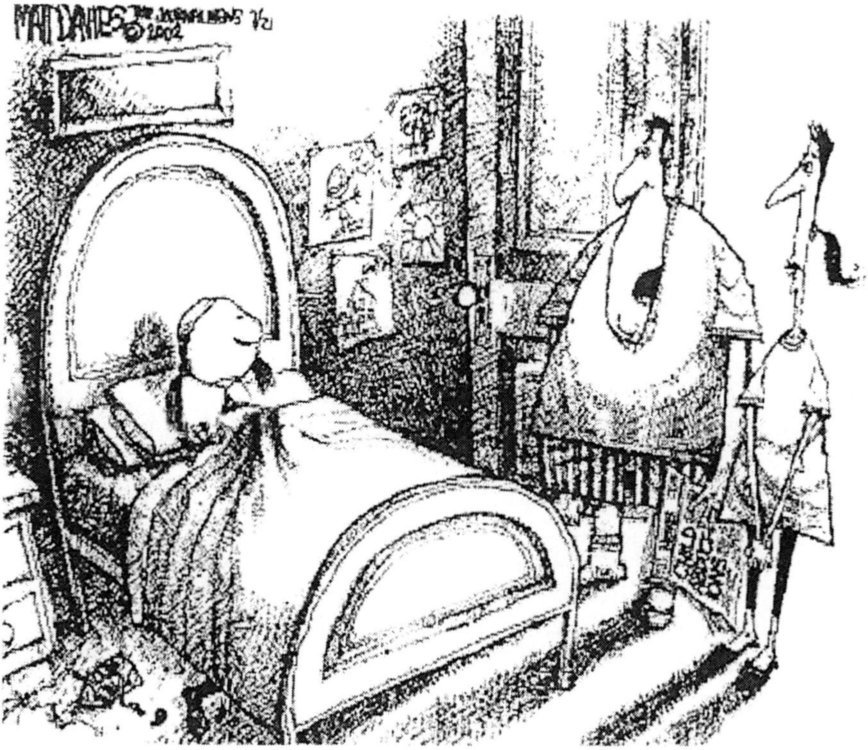

"WE'RE SCARED...CAN YOU SLEEP IN OUR BED??"

APPENDIX
SAFETY TIPS FOR PARENTS

When I first decided to write this book, I only intended to capture the attention of the parents so that they could learn how to protect their children, and empower them to become more safe and confident.

However, as I was writing the draft, my wife asked, "Why don't you include a chapter specifically for the parents?"

At first I was a little hesitant, because I didn't want to offend anyone by suggesting that they did not know how to protect themselves; but then I thought of Ted Bundy. He was a handsome, well-educated man who played on women's natural sympathies by pretending he was a disabled person needing assistance. Stopping to help this man was the last decision these kind, unsuspecting women made. Ted Bundy confessed to killing 28 women, however, others estimate that as many as 33 to 100 other women became victims to his ploy, making him one of the most infamous serial killers in America. If you look at it from that point of view, there is no way I could not listen to my wonderful wife.

Although I am only 40-years-old, I've lived back in the days of no cell phones. Now it seems like we can't live without them. Actually, in today's world, you would be foolish not to have a cell phone, and have 911 programmed into speed dial.

When I do safety programs for realtors, that's the first thing I tell them. When you are in a situation where you are by yourself, such as in a bad neighborhood, in an unfamiliar location, out at night, etc., you should have the cell phone in hand and 911 on speed dial. It's a lot easier to hit one button under stress than three. One of the most important things you must learn is to always trust your instincts/intuitions, rather than dismissing them.

When it comes to safety, basically the same rules apply for adults as they do for children. Research shows, however, that with adults, our appearance means a lot more than it does with kids. Attackers tend to be drawn to women with ponytails or buns, rather than women with short hair, and they also look for women who wear clothes that are easily and quickly removed.

I strongly believe that the A, B, C, And D's of self-defense should carry over for adults as well. The attacker is always looking for the weak and timid victim - a submissive person who will not put up much of a fight. Remember, the more alert and confident you appear; the less likely it is that you will become a victim.

The following is a list of crucial tips for adults - especially women - to follow in emergency situations:

1. **A stranger approaches and asks for assistance. STOP AND THINK before you act.** Women especially must use head over heart to prevent being victimized. It's unfortunate, but in today's world, we have to think before rendering assistance. If being a Good Samaritan could get you killed, it's not worth it. If someone approaches you, stop at a distance to think about the situation and your surroundings. Ask yourself if helping this person will, in any way, put you at risk. If so, then STOP. Do not compromise your boundaries. Walk away. Period.

2. **a) You are abducted and thrown into the <u>trunk</u> of a car.** Remember: it is not over yet. Kick out the tail lights of the vehicle and stick your arms out of the hole, and start waving like crazy. The bad guy/driver cannot see you doing this, and, hopefully, everyone else will. Another thing to remember is that most newer cars have either a trap door in the trunk that

will allow access to the back seat, or there will be a pull lever to unlock the trunk latch from the inside. Search until you find the latch, and come out with the tire iron in your hand!

b) If you are abducted and thrown into the passenger seat of a car, ***remember, the only thing you cannot do is give up!*** You can jump out of the car or grab the steering wheel, causing the driver to crash. You can turn the keys off and break the key in the ignition. You can beep the horn, scratch his eyes, hit him in the groin...anything to draw attention to you and provide a chance of escape.

3. One question I hear pretty often is, **"What should I do when I approach my vehicle?"** This is a good question. It goes back to the basic "A" in self-defense: **Awareness. You should be aware of your surroundings as you approach your car.** Be alert - have your keys already in your hand, and look into your vehicle, at the passenger side floor, and in the back seat before entering your vehicle. One thing that the bad guy is looking for is the person who is walking to her car, talking on the cell phone, or doing some other activity while walking. This person is off guard, distracted, and can easily be overpowered.

4. **If you are parked next to a van on the driver's side of your vehicle, enter your vehicle on the passenger side**. Most serial killers or abductors attack their victims by pulling them into a van. Another thing to watch out for is a male sitting alone in the passenger seat of a car, which is parked on your driver's side. Should this be the case, you may want to return to where you just came from, and get an escort back to your vehicle. **It is always better to be safe than sorry...do not let potential embarrassment lead to your rape or death.**

5. **Another way to be safe while approaching and entering**

your car/vehicle, if you have a newer auto, is to use the automatic door opener. This can help you in two ways. First, it allows you to enter your vehicle without taking the time to use the key to unlock the door; and secondly, it automatically turns on the interior light, giving you an opportunity to see if anyone is hiding in your car. For the automatic door openers alone, it would not be a bad idea to upgrade to a newer car if you have not already done so. Another advantage to this is the reduced likelihood of your car breaking down, placing you at risk.

6. **If an abductor does jump in your car and tells you to drive**, there's nothing saying that you cannot drive your car into another parked car or into a fixed object in order to gain attention and end the ride. This may be your last chance to survive, so don't worry about hurting your car or someone else's. That's what you pay insurance for.

7. **Do not sit and work in a parked car.** It's easy to do: you've just finished shopping and you need to make a call or subtract your checkbook, etc., but resist the urge. The bad guy/predator will be watching you, and this gives him a perfect opportunity to jump into the passenger side of your vehicle, put a gun to your head, and tell you to drive. Prevent this situation from happening...get in your vehicle, lock your doors, and leave the area immediately.

8. **A robber approaches and asks for your wallet or purse.** Do not stand and argue with him, and don't just give it to him - toss the thing just a few feet away from you, and run like crazy in the opposite direction, yelling for help in order to draw attention to yourself. Hopefully the bad guy will be more interested in the purse/wallet than in you.

9. **Use the elevator instead of the stairs.** Stairwells are a

horrible place to be alone and the perfect place for a crime, especially at night.

10. **If the bad guy has a gun and you are not under his control, *always run*, and always run in a zigzag pattern.** The bad guy will have a lot harder time hitting a moving target than if you just give up!

11. The last and most important rule goes back to the protection of your child. ***NEVER, EVER*** leave your child alone in a car. This is the fastest way to have your child abducted/ kidnapped. I know what you are going to say, "...I'll only be a second, and I don't want to wake the baby up, she just feel asleep..." The one time you take a chance and leave your child alone in the car, could very well be the last.

By now, you may be afraid to leave your house. That is not my attention, but a little fear is a good thing if you use it to be smart - to motivate yourself to take the actions I've suggested to protect yourself and your family.

You know the old saying, "Prevention is the best medicine." Hopefully, none of these scary situations will ever happen to you, or anyone you love. But, if and when an attempted abduction does take place, it should be comforting to know that you are now armed with some knowledge and techniques that give you and yours a fighting chance.

AFTERWORD

I hope that after reading this book, you will feel empowered to teach your children to become safer. The gift of life is the most precious gift of all and we must do everything we can to protect and preserve it. We all want the best for our children and it is our job to see to it that they have every opportunity to enjoy life and to make the best of it.

I have thoroughly enjoyed writing this book and sharing my Law Enforcement and Martial Arts experiences and knowledge with you. After all, what's the sense of having information if you cannot share it with others? There is no more joy in life than teaching children and seeing that light bulb go on when they finally understand what you are saying.

As you have read, tools and techniques do exist that can increase the chances of your children staying safe in an abduction situation. The next step is up to you. Do what I have done and pass this information forward: to your children, your children's friends and parents, your coworkers, your neighbors…anyone, anytime you can. Together we can help put those predators out of business, and keep our children safe.

ABOUT THE AUTHOR

James Giammarinaro (known to all his colleagues as G-11, in deference to the number of letters in his family name) began his Law Enforcement career in 1990, with the St. Augustine, Florida Police Department. Although he always wanted to be a policeman, Jim had no real direction or field expertise beyond his desire to make a positive difference in the world.

After ten years of street-earned experience, James became a detective within his department. It didn't take long for him to create a name for himself. Shortly after becoming a detective, G-11 began working a thirty-year-old homicide case, which he solved. This breakthrough started a whirlwind of media frenzy, culminating in his being featured on the popular TV show, *Cold Case Files.* Many of you have probably seen Detective Giammarinaro in this episode, without realizing it was him.

As a result of this initial digging, James found that his passion was in the field of cold-case homicides, and was fueled by his strong belief that people should be held accountable for their actions, that nobody should get away with murder, and that the victims and their families deserve justice.

During these years, James' family grew to include three children of his own, whom he loves, adores and wants to protect from the predators he knows inhabit his world on the street. Wanting to educate children about the potential dangers that stalk them on the streets, he and his department's Public Information Officer developed St. Augustine's first ever Situational Awareness Seminars. He first began presenting the program in the county school system. The stark realism of the information presented, and the obvious practical benefit to those children who saw it, created a tremendous demand for additional Situational Awareness Seminars throughout the community.

Wanting to expand the universe of children he could potentially help, and anguished by seeing so many children needlessly abducted and murdered, G-11 decided to write this book, ***Parents, Predators, and Prevention***.

In creating this book, Detective Giammarinaro has called upon his seventeen years of Law Enforcement experience, combined it with his Situational Awareness Seminars, and enhanced it with his eleven years of Martial Arts experience (James is a Third Degree Black Belt Instructor in TaeKwonDo).

The results are now in... ***Parents, Predators, and Prevention*** is the most complete guide available for parents to use in the education of their children, increasing their chances to live a safer and more confident life.

James continues to catch the bad guys, and to present his Situational Awareness Seminars in Saint Augustine; and St. Johns County, Florida, is now a much safer community because of his efforts.

I would love to hear from readers, so please visit the website: www.childsafetyteam.com

Child Safety Team, Inc.

The original publication of *Parents, Predators and Prevention* brought to light the need for a further expansion of programs teaching Situational Awareness and Safety from Predators; so James and his wife opened a 501(c)(3) non-profit organization, Child Safety Team, Inc. to fulfill this need.

The Child Safety Team offers Situational Awareness & Safety Seminars for children, Women's Self-Defense Courses, and Adult Safety Seminars.

The Child Safety Team, through grants and private funding, purchases copies of *Parents, Predators and Prevention* and donates them to families who participate in their Situational Awareness & Safety Seminars.

Sergeant James Giammarinaro and the Board of Directors of Child Safety Team, Inc. vow to stay aggressive and proactive in the fight to keep our precious kids safe, but we cannot do it alone. Through your generous donations we can continue to expand our programs and reach out to more people.

If you would like to make a donation that could truly make the difference in the life of a child, you can mail a check or money order to:

The Child Safety Team, Inc.
4436 Eagle Creek Court
Elkton, FL 32033

All donations are ***tax deductible***
and a receipt will be emailed or mailed for all donations.

Make check payable to:
The Child Safety Team, Inc.

REFERENCES

Abduction Cartoons, Internet Broadcasting Systems, Inc., WJXT-Channel 4, news4jax.com; Jacksonville, FL, 2004.

Amber Alert (America's Missing Broadcast Emergency Response), US Department of Justice, Office of Juvenile Justice and Delinquency Prevention (www.ojp.usdoj.gov); www.amberalert.gov, Washington, DC, 2001.

Association of Missing and Exploited Children's Organization (Ameco), 320-363-0470, www.amecoinc.org; Alexandria, VA.

Beyond Missing, Inc. founded by Marc Klaas, partially funded by a US Department of Justice, Office of Justice Program grant (OJJDP), 415-461-(find) 3463; www.beyondmissing.com; Sausalito, CA.

Frequently Asked Questions & Statistics Web Pages, National Center for Missing and Exploited Children, www.missingkids.com; Alexandria, Virginia; 2006.

Internet Security Companies:

- www.cyberangels.com, Cyber Angels, Allentown, PA.
- www.cyberpatrol.com, Surf Control, Inc., Westborough, MA.
- www.Symantec.com, Symantec, Cupertino, CA.

Lanning, Kenneth V., *Child Molesters: A Behavioral Analysis, 4th Edition; Publication for Law Enforcement*; US Deparment of Justice, Office of Juvenile Justice and Delinquency Prevention; www.ojp.usdoj.gov; Washington, DC, 2001.

Martin, Craig, Video 1 - *Becoming Aware;* Video Two - *Taking Action*; Kidz 'n Power; Worthridge, California; www.kidznpower.com; July, 2004.

Martinez, Marilyn, and Walker, Natalie; *Keeping Kids Safe on the Internet* Web Page; Parents Guide Press, www.parenthood.com, 2003.

National Center for Missing and Exploited Children (NCMEC); 800-THE-LOST, www.missingkids.com; Alexandria, Virginia; 2006.

National Incidence Studies of Missing, Abducted, Runaway, and Thrownaway Children (NISMART-2, statistics from 1999, released in October 2002), Office of Juvenile Justice and Delinquency Prevention; www.ojp.usdoj.gov; Washington, DC.

Safe Steps Iniative, Office of the Attorney General of Florida, National Center for Missing and Exploited Children, Florida School Boards Association, Macy's and Royal Caribbean Cruises Ltd., Tallahassee, FL, www.safestepsfla.net, 2006.

Safe Steps Poll, Mason-Dixon Polling & Research, Inc. of Washington, D.C., June, 2006.

Sex Offender Registries:

-State of Florida: www.fdle.state.fl.us.

-National Sex Offender Registry: wwwnsopr.gov.

-www.familywatchdog.us and click on 'Find Offenders.'

Index

W

Y

Breinigsville, PA USA
26 October 2009

226520BV00002B/6/P

9 781888 562187